# BHARATPUR

*Bird Paradise*

# BHARA

TEXT
**Martin Ewans**
PHOTOGRAPHS
**Thakur Dalip Singh, Rajpal Singh,
James Hancock & others**

# TPUR

# Bird Paradise

H.F. & G. WITHERBY LTD.

*for Mary*

First published in Great Britain 1989
by H.F. & G. Witherby Ltd.
14 Henrietta Street,
London WC2E 8QJ

Text © Martin Ewans
Photographs © Thakur Dalip Singh,
Rajpal Singh, James Hancock,
M.Y. Ghorpade, P. Evans,
W.S. Paton, Rupin Dang, Mike Price,
M.M. Singh, P. Kapoor, Joanna Van Gruisen
(Photo credits on page 144)

Designed by Priyadarshi

British Library Cataloguing
in Publication Data
Ewans, Martin
Bharatpur bird paradise
1. (Republic) India. Bharatpur.
Bird sanctuaries.
Bharatpur Bird Reserve
I. Title
639.9'782 9543

ISBN O-85493-163-5

Photoset in ITC Garamond by Lustre Print Media Pvt. Ltd., New Delhi

Printed and bound by Tien Wah Press (Pte) Ltd., Singapore

# CONTENTS

# PREFACE

IT IS well-nigh impossible to live in India and not be conscious of the immense variety of its birdlife. Vultures and pariah kites are all too apt to greet the very aircraft in which one arrives, and are an obtrusive feature of every Indian city and town. Crows, babblers, bulbuls, robins, mynahs, doves and many more throng every garden; peafowl and parakeets add noise and colour to fields and villages. It has been reckoned that no less than 1,200 species in over 2,000 forms have been identified over the years at some place or other in the Indian sub-continent.

Nowhere in India, and perhaps nowhere in Asia, does so spectacular a concourse of birds gather as in the Keoladeo Ghana National Park near Bharatpur in Rajasthan state, not far from Delhi. The aim of this book is to give some account of this Park and of some of the species of birds which are to be found in it. It is, inevitably, a selective and impressionistic work, designed to present an overall picture rather than a detailed inventory. To produce the latter would be an abstruse and massive undertaking, and the result would be likely to resemble a handbook of Indian birds, of which several impressive examples already exist, the most notable being the magisterial 10-volume *Handbook of the Birds of India and Pakistan* by Salim Ali and S. Dillon Ripley. Rather, the intention is to give the general reader a broad idea of what he will most easily see if he should have the good fortune to visit this paradise—the home, permanent or seasonal, of well over three hundred species of birds, ranging from the magnificent Sarus and Siberian Cranes and ten species of eagles at one extreme, to a wide variety of passerines at the other.

There is also another aim. As I shall explain, Bharatpur exists precariously, and pressures on it have been building up over several years. At the time of writing, the chances of its survival are again threatened and it can by no means be assumed that it will survive indefinitely. If this book should help in any measure to extend interest and concern, and to support and encourage those many people, both in India and further afield, who have been working assiduously to secure the future of Bharatpur, I shall be more than content.

No book about Indian birds can fail to be massively indebted to Dr Salim Ali, the veteran Indian ornithologist whose vast knowledge and lively sense of purpose combined to give him a pre-eminent—and worldwide—reputation in this field. His recent death is a grievous loss to friends and ornithologists alike. I must also express my appreciation for the friendly hospitality accorded to me by the Rajasthan Forests Department, and in particular by the Deputy Chief Wildlife Warden at Bharatpur, Mr Bholu Abrar Khan and his staff.

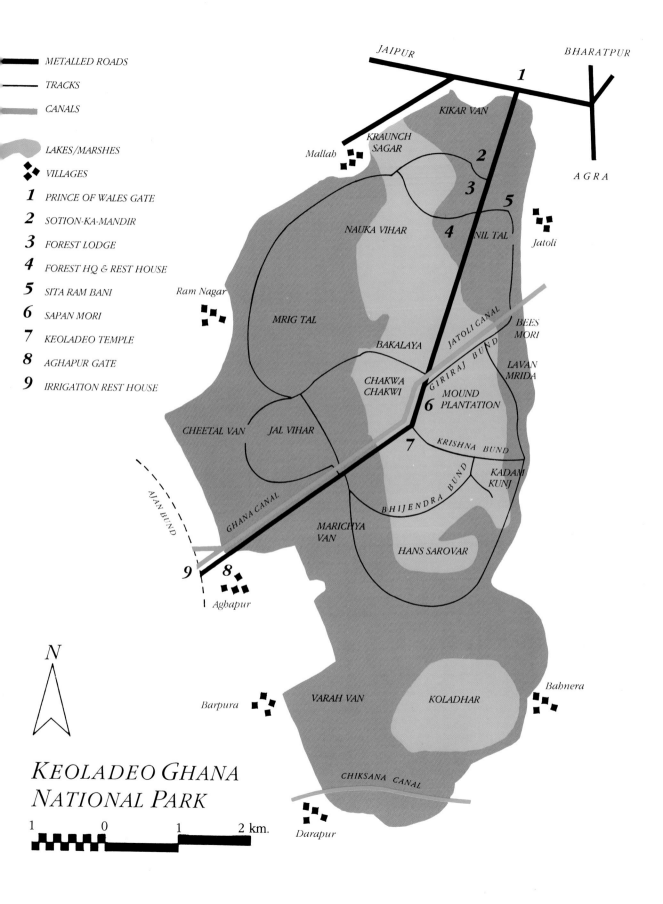

KEOLADEO GHANA NATIONAL PARK

JAIPUR  BHARATPUR

**1** PRINCE OF WALES GATE

*Mallah*

KIKAR VAN

KRAUNCH SAGAR

**2** SOTION-KA-MANDIR

**3** FOREST LODGE

NAUKA VIHAR

**4** FOREST HQ & REST HOUSE

**5**  ANIL TAL

*Jatoli*

**5** SITA RAM BANI

*Ram Nagar*

MRIG TAL

JATOLI CANAL

BEES MORI

**6** SAPAN MORI

BAKALAYA

GIRIRAJ BUND

LAVAN MRIDA

**7** KEOLADEO TEMPLE

CHAKWA CHAKWI

**6** MOUND PLANTATION

CHEETAL VAN

JAL VIHAR

**7**

KRISHNA BUND

KADAM KUNJ

**8** AGHAPUR GATE

AJAN BUND

GHANA CANAL

BHIJENDRA BUND

**9** IRRIGATION REST HOUSE

MARICHYA VAN

HANS SAROVAR

**9**  **8**

*Aghapur*

N

*Barpura*

VARAH VAN

KOLADHAR

*Bahnera*

CHIKSANA CANAL

*Darapur*

LEGEND

METALLED ROADS

TRACKS

CANALS

LAKES/MARSHES

VILLAGES

1  0  1  2 km.

# BHARATPUR
# AN INTRODUCTION

T O THE immediate south of the Indian capital, Delhi, lies an area of country which is known in tourist circles as the 'Golden Triangle'. Its south-east limits are marked by Agra, of Taj Mahal and Mughal fame, and the south-west by Jaipur, the 'Pink City', capital of the state of Rajasthan. It is a stretch of flat, featureless alluvial plain, bounded on the east by the river Jamuna, a major tributary of the Ganga, and on the west by a range of ancient, worn-down hills, the Aravallis. It is mostly agricultural land, patterned with a host of villages and many small towns. Except on the hills, to the west, there is little or no forest. Intensive farming, mostly of wheat, sugarcane and rice, provides a living for the countrymen of Rajasthan, Haryana and western Uttar Pradesh, the three states which impinge on the area.

The traveller who takes the road westwards from Agra, along the base of the triangle, will reach within a short while the hilltop city of Fatehpur Sikri, built in impressive style by the Mughal emperor Akbar in the sixteenth century, but abandoned after only a few years' occupation. A few miles on lies Bharatpur, one of the easternmost towns of Rajasthan and formerly a Jat princely state. The Jats are a tough farming people who still play a role in Indian politics: one of their leaders was Prime Minister of India for a few months in 1979. Bharatpur itself was carved out as an independent state in the late seventeenth century, and in the following century the Jat rulers were powerful enough to hold Agra for some years and even to sack Delhi. Later in the eighteenth century Jat power began to decline until, after two sieges in the early nineteenth century, the state was brought to heel by the British. At Independence in 1947 the state was incorporated into the Indian Union, and a few years later the ruling family, so powerful in their day, became private citizens.

It was one of the Maharajas of Bharatpur who was responsible during the 1890s for the creation of what is now the Keoladeo Ghana National Park. Conservation was a concept which of course had little or no currency at that time: rather the contrary. Inspired by a visit to Britain, in the course of which he was invited to shoots of wildfowl by his English hosts, the Maharaja was moved to create his own

Title page: *Rosy Pelicans* (Pelecanus onocrotalus) *are highly gregarious and fly, feed and breed in large groups. Their method of fishing is to swim together in horse-shoe formation, dipping their wide-open mouths into the water at intervals so that their gular pouches function as a solid underwater 'net' which scoops up any fish in range.* [See pg. 62]

Contents page: *The Indian Bay-backed Shrike* (Lanius vittatus) *is a small but ferocious bird which preys on large and small insects, caterpillars, lizards, young mice and even fledgling birds. Like other shrikes, it has the habit of storing its prey impaled on thorns or barbed wire, for which reason it is known as the 'Butcher Bird'.*

Preface: *The Indian River Tern* (Sterna aurantia) *is an elegant flier with long, pointed wings and a forked tail. It is widely found around large rivers, estuaries and tanks rich in fish, crustaceans and aquatic insects on which it feeds. It hunts singly or in twos or threes, diving into the water from a height with wings folded.*

| DATE | ON THE OCCASION OF THE VISIT OF | BAG | GUNS |
|---|---|---|---|
| 1902 1ST DEC | 1ST SHOOT H E VICEROY LORD CURZON H.E.C-IN C LORD KITCHENER | 540 | 17 |
| 1903 9TH FEB | 2ND SHOOT H.R.H. THE DUKE OF CANNAUGHT | 780 | 19 |
| 1903 14TH DEC | 1ST SHOOT H.E. VICEROY LORD CURZON | 2049 | 45 |
| 1907 15TH NOV | 1ST SHOOT HON'BLE MR E. COLVIN A.G.G. | 1750 | 32 |
| 1908 30TH NOV | 1ST SHOOT HON'BLE COL. PINNEY A.G.G. | 2141 | 33 |
| 1908 12TH NOV | 2ND SHOOT | 1085 | 27 |
| 1909 27TH NOV | 1ST SHOOT HON'BLE MR E.COLVIN A.G.G. | 3297 | 48 |
| 1909 24TH DEC | 2ND SHOOT | 504 | 20 |
| 1910 4TH JAN | 3RD SHOOT | 664 | 24 |
| 1910 1ST DEC | 1ST SHOOT H.H. MAHARAJA BIKANER | 2758 | 51 |
| 1910 31ST DEC | 2ND SHOOT H.I.H.THE CROWN PRINCE OF GERMANY | 1379 | 49 |
| 1911 13TH FEB | 3RD SHOOT H.H.MAHARAJ RANA OF DHOLPUR | 1712 | 42 |
| 1911 8TH NOV | H.H. MAHARAJA BIKANER H.H.MAHARAJ RANA OF DHOLPUR | 1285 | 48 |
| 1911 30TH DEC | 2ND SHOOT H.H.MAHARAJA'S 1ST SHOOT | 1022 | 29 |
| 1912 20TH JAN | 3RD SHOOT H.H.MAHARAJA KISHENGARH | 1439 | 41 |
| 1912 15TH FEB | 4TH SHOOT HON'BLE MR.R.E.HOLLAND | 1317 | 27 |
| 1912 5TH NOV | 1ST SHOOT MAHARAJ RANA DHOLPUR | 716 | 16 |
| 1912 21ST DEC | 2ND SHOOT H.E.VICEROY LORD HARDING | 3511 | 51 |

*Bharatpur came into existence in the 1890s chiefly as a private game reserve of the then Maharaja, to which he could invite shooting parties of British and Indian notables. A tally engraved on stone plaques records the slaughter of game birds over the first half of this century.*

| DATE | ON THE OCCASION OF THE VISIT OF | BAG | GUNS |
|---|---|---|---|
| 1913 31ST JAN | 3RD SHOOT HON'BLE MR MONTAGUE | 2122 | 40 |
| 1913 8TH FEB | 4TH SHOOT | 405 | 13 |
| 1913 15TH OCT | AJAN BUND H.H.MAHARAJ RANA DHOLPUR | 935 | 17 |
| 1913 3RD DEC | 1ST SHOOT H.E.VICEROY LORD HARDING | 4062 | 49 |
| 1915 30TH JAN | 2ND SHOOT H.H.MAHARAJA PATIALA | 2433 | 38 |
| 1915 13TH NOV | 1ST SHOOT H.E.VICEROY LORD HARDING | 1715 | 30 |
| 1915 30TH NOV | 2ND SHOOT H.H.MAHARAJ RANA DHOLPUR | 942 | 13 |
| 1916 20TH NOV | 1ST SHOOT H.E.VICEROY LORD CHELMSFORD | 4206 | 50 |
| 1917 8TH JAN | 2ND SHOOT HON'BLE SIR ELLIOT COLVIN A.G.G. | 1805 | 24 |
| 1917 30TH JAN | 3RD SHOOT HON'BLE MAHARAJA FARIDKOT | 710 | 18 |
| 1918 12TH JAN | 1ST SHOOT H.E.VICEROY LORD CHELMSFORD | 2666 | 25 |
| 1918 23RD FEB | 2ND SHOOT SECRETARY OF STATE RT. HON'BLE MR MONTAGUE | 1314 | 26 |
| 1918 30TH NOV | 1ST SHOOT HON'BLE COL— | 2411 | 33 |
| 1918 21ST DEC | 2ND SHOOT H.H.MAHARAJ RANA DHOLPUR | 1084 | 33 |
| 1919 27TH DEC | 1ST SHOOT COL. BANNERMAN | 3041 | 51 |
| 1920 31ST JAN | 2ND SHOOT HIS HIGHNESS' SHOOT | 2659 | 42 |
| 1920 11TH MAR | 3RD SHOOT | 1507 | 30 |
| 1920 28TH OCT | 1ST SHOOT DASHERA SHOOT H.E.SIR GEORGE LOYD H.E.SIR HERCORT BUTLER SIR HERWARD WAKE | 587 | 51 |

reserve, at which he could in turn play host to British and Indian notables. To do so, he deepened and extended an area of existing marshland, to increase its attraction for wildfowl, and made it accessible through the construction of dykes and tracks. The undertaking was a great success, and the numbers of duck slaughtered each year was prodigious. A tally, which is engraved on stone plaques still standing in the heart of the Park, was kept each year over the first half of this century. It shows, for example, that in 1938 a shooting party headed by the then Viceroy of India, Lord Linlithgow, downed no less than 4,273 birds in a single day. Between 1907 and 1946 there were nineteen shoots in which more than 2,000 birds were shot, and of these there were five in which the bag numbered more than 3,000.

Shooting last took place at Bharatpur in 1964, but even in the previous decade a start had been made in managing the area as a sanctuary. It was Dr Salim Ali who first saw its great importance and campaigned for its creation. Since 1956 the maintenance of the sanctuary at Bharatpur has been the responsibility of the Rajasthan Forests Department, and in August 1981 it was declared a National Park.

# The Park

Bharatpur is thus a largely artificial creation. The Maharaja enclosed a large area with embankments and divided it with further 'bunds' to create a number of separate lakes and marshes. It is therefore possible to reach the greater part of the sanctuary on foot or by jeep, and yet the marshes are large enough, if left undisturbed, to provide a sufficiently safe refuge for a host of wildfowl and larger birds. The Park covers some 29 square kilometres in all. Much of it is marsh, but it also contains substantial areas of semi-arid woodland and scrub. Towards the south of the Park, the scrub gradually thins out and gives way to a broad expanse of grassland, studded with a few groves of mature trees and surrounding a further area of swamp and reedbeds. This is Koladahar, a haunt of the elegant Black Buck; of larks, chats and buntings; of the Short-toed Eagle and Black-winged Kite; of sandgrouse and pratincoles; and, in the reedbeds, of herons, egrets and storks. The commonest trees in the Park are Babul (*Acacia nilotica*) and Ber (*Zizyphus jujuba*), added to which are scattered Kadam (*Mitragyna parvifolia*) and Peepul (*Ficus religiosa*). There are also two exotic species, Vilayati Babul (*Prosopis juliflora*) and Besharam (*Ipoemea carnea*), both of which are spreading rapidly and altering for the worse the Park's eco-system.

The Park is dependent partly on rainfall for the maintenance of its lakes and vegetation, and partly on artificial irrigation. In a normal year the inundated areas start to refill with the onset of the monsoon in July, August and September. Further water comes by canal from a large irrigation work, the Ajan Bund, to the west of the Park. This also fills up during the monsoon and a considerable head of water forms behind its twelve miles of length. Part of this is released through sluices for the benefit of neighbouring farmland, but the greater part is fed through a canal into the Park and, through smaller sluices, into the various marshes. Over the rest of the year the Park gradually dries out, until replenished by the following monsoon. Without the supply from the Ajan Bund, there would be far from sufficient water to preserve the marshland throughout the year; the maintenance and use of the irrigation system is thus essential for the survival of the Park.

Every so often in India, a year of a weak monsoon brings widespread drought. 1979 and 1987 were years in which the Bharatpur sanctuary largely lost its natural replenishment of water, and was barely kept alive only by assiduous pumping from several tube wells. A remarkable feature after 1979 was the recovery in numbers, both of birds and of fish, but the drought of 1987 seems to have been even more severe, and the extent to which the Park will recover remains to be seen.

# The Seasons at Bharatpur

Bharatpur is a delight at any time of the year, but it has two special seasons. The first is the monsoon, which is the breeding season for many of the resident or locally migrant birds. The other is winter, when the long-distance migrants come. Many of the residents breed quietly and even secretively at various times of the year. However, the filling of the lakes in the monsoon is the signal for several of the more spectacular species to converge on Bharatpur. The first to arrive are the Open-bill Storks, but soon the trees are full of a variety of nesting birds, egrets, herons, cormorants, Open-bill and Painted Storks, ibises and Spoonbills. The Painted Storks frequently congregate by themselves, but sometimes they nest with others and, in many trees, several species settle cheek by jowl. An estimate made by the Park Warden is that some 44,000 trees are used for nesting purposes each year.

At first the nesting trees are strangely silent. There is to be heard only the rattle of beaks and flapping of wings as the birds establish territories, settle themselves, build their nests and incubate their eggs. Nest building and repair seem to consist as much of filching twigs from other birds' nests as of finding new material. There is an air of muted concern as the birds both forage for food and protect their nests from ever-threatening raptors and crows. Occasionally there is a tragedy, as parental watchfulness falters and a predator snatches a hasty meal. At dawn and dusk thousands of birds ply to and from the

| DATE | ON THE OCCASION OF THE VISIT OF | BAG | GUNS |
|---|---|---|---|
| 1921 8th DEC | 2nd SHOOT H.R.H.THE PRINCE OF WALES | 2221 | 53 |
| 1922 25th NOV | 1st SHOOT H.E.VICEROY LORD READING | 984 | 32 |
| 1922 6th DEC | 2nd SHOOT H.E.LORD LYTTON LORD INCHCAPE | 792 | 40 |
| 1923 28th JAN | 3rd SHOOT | 365 | 16 |
| 1923 25th FEB | 4th SHOOT H.E.VICEROY LORD READING | 732 | 32 |
| 1923 8th NOV | 1st SHOOT H.E.THE C-IN-C LORD RAWLINSON | 2126 | 57 |
| 1924 27th JAN | 2nd SHOOT H.E.VICEROY LORD READING | 3443 | 60 |
| 1924 22nd NOV | 1st SHOOT H.E.THE C-IN-C LORD RAWLINSON | 335 | 21 |
| 1925 10th FEB | 2nd SHOOT H.E.VICEROY LORD READING | 865 | 36 |
| 1925 28th FEB | 3rd SHOOT | 1388 | 38 |
| 1925 22nd MAR | 4th SHOOT H.H MAHARAJA ALWAR | 1001 | 38 |
| 1925 6th DEC | 1st SHOOT RAMBAGH | 289 | 8 |
| 1925 26th DEC | 2nd SHOOT XMAS SHOOT | 945 | 23 |
| 1926 2nd DEC | 1st SHOOT T.H.THE MAHARAJAS OF PATIALA,DHOLPUR,ALWAR, BHOPAL,RUTLAM & MUNDI | 2316 | 60 |

*Shooting last took place at Bharatpur in 1964, but had been curtailed earlier when the Park was accorded the status of a sanctuary. In 1981, as a result of campaigning by conservationists and ornithologists, chiefly Dr Salim Ali, the sanctuary was declared a National Park.*

| DATE | ON THE OCCASION OF THE VISIT OF :- | BAG | GUNS |
|---|---|---|---|
| 1927 17th NOV | 1st SHOOT H.H MAHARAJA ALWAR | 1453 | 51 |
| 1927 17th DEC | 2nd SHOOT H.H.MAHARAJA ALWAR | 1016 | 49 |
| 1932 12th NOV | 1st SHOOT | 1460 | 44 |
| 1932 10th DEC | 2nd SHOOT | 725 | 26 |
| 1933 18th NOV | 1st SHOOT | 862 | 46 |
| 1933 9th DEC | 2nd SHOOT | 515 | 45 |
| 1934 4th FEB | 3rd SHOOT | 363 | 44 |
| 1934 17th NOV | 1st SHOOT | 1557 | 45 |
| 1934 8th DEC | 2nd SHOOT | 1035 | 33 |
| 1935 9th FEB | 3rd SHOOT | 1235 | 35 |
| 1935 9th NOV | 1st SHOOT | 1357 | 43 |
| 1935 7th DEC | 2nd SHOOT | 1615 | 44 |
| 1936 8th FEB | 3rd SHOOT | 1683 | 44 |
| 1936 9th NOV | H.E.THE VICEROY LORD LINLITHGOW | 1415 | 50 |
| 1936 5th DEC | 2nd SHOOT | 1476 | 41 |
| 1937 6th FEB | 3rd SHOOT | 2588 | 39 |
| 1938 ?th NOV | VISIT OF H.E. THE VICEROY LORD LINLITHGOW MORNING 3044 AFTERNOON 1229 | 4273 | 39 |
| 1938 4th DEC | 2nd SHOOT CENTRAL INDIA HORSE | 2054 | 32 |

Opposite: *The Crimson-breasted Barbet* (Megalaima haemacephala) *is also known as the Coppersmith because of its monotonous metallic note. It is common and very widespread, generally in forest or lightly wooded areas. It eats wild berries, figs and drupes, but is occasionally insectivorous.*

Top: *The Black Drongo* (Dicrurus adsimilis), *commonly resident in the sub-continent, is an arboreal and wholly carnivorous bird which feeds on insects and vermin. Its Hindi name Kotwal, 'sentinel', refers to the Drongo's vigilance against intruders.* [See pg. 104]

Bottom: *The Red-vented Bulbul* (Pycnonotus cafer) *is a common resident, in former*

[Continued overleaf]

[Contd.] *times trained as a fighting bird. It used to be fed on a special diet to enhance its pugnacity, and fights often culminated in the death of one or both birds.*

Top: *The Red-wattled Lapwing* (Vanellus indicus) *is widely resident in the country in the neighbourhood of water, usually feeding at the water's edge in the evenings or at night. This wader is an irritant to sportsmen on account of its loud screams which alert game birds to the proximity of danger.*

marshes to seek food from the surrounding countryside.

The atmosphere changes, however, once the eggs begin to hatch. The air becomes filled with the noise of hungry nestlings and parental activity multiplies. Fishing takes place on a huge scale, with egrets and cormorants traversing the marshes in flocks, driving the fish before them. The impression given by a flock of egrets on the hunt is of a creeping barrage, with the birds at the rear flying constantly across the flock and becoming the new vanguard. Eagles and harriers glide overhead, seeking opportunity to snatch an unguarded fledgling. Over the weeks the young birds grow and progressively depart, the last to leave being the Painted Storks, whose relatively dull offspring hang around the nests until well into the autumn and winter. Finally, as the water level in the marshes drops and nesting is complete, most of the birds fly out from Bharatpur to seek more plentiful sources of food in rivers and lakes elsewhere.

With the winter come the migrants. Perhaps to a greater extent than many places, Bharatpur arouses a sense of awe at the perennial wonder of bird migration. The migrants mostly come from Eastern Europe, Siberia or Central Asia, often over distances of several thousands of miles. They navigate with pin-point accuracy, reaching this tiny speck within the vast Gangetic plain year after year. They include not just the large birds such as storks and cranes, geese and ducks, but also many smaller species. The Black-headed Bunting

Top: *The Indian Little Ringed Plover* (Charadrius dubius), *a highly migratory bird, exhibits the rounded body, disruptive plumage and long wings typical of waders.*

Bottom: *The Common Teal* (Anas crecca) *is a widespread winter visitor to India from its home in the Caspian region and Siberia. Its annual arrival is keenly awaited by huntsmen on account of its sporting qualities as well as its virtues as a table bird. The green metallic eye-to-nape band and tricoloured wing bar identify this specimen as a male.*

*Young egrets obtain their food by the curious method of gripping the parental beak aggressively and almost wrestling the regurgitated fish out of it.* [See pg. 45]

(*Emberiza melanocephala*), for example, will have travelled up to 6,500 kilometres in its journey from its breeding grounds in south-eastern Europe and the Mediterranean; while the recovery has been recorded in Kazakhstan, during the summer, of Spanish and Turkestan Sparrows (*Passer hispaniolensis transcaspicus* and *P. domesticus bactrianus*) ringed at Bharatpur in early spring. The main migration routes into India run down the valleys of the Indus in the west and the Brahmaputra in the east, but there is also good evidence that many birds fly straight over the Himalayas or the Hindu Kush.

Why birds migrate across Asia needs little explanation. As the Siberian winter closes in, both the accessibility of food and the daylight hours available for finding it diminish, and this is probably as compelling a factor in instigating movement as the intense cold and the rigours of snow and ice which follow. Conversely, the difficulties of surviving, and still more of raising offspring, in the heat of the Indian summer and the deluges of the monsoon, need little imagination. Birds such as the Painted Stork which are adapted to breeding in India have to spend hours each day with outstretched wings, sheltering their nestlings from the searing heat. At the same time, Siberia is enjoying long daylight hours in which foraging can take place, and food is then abundant.

How the birds migrate over these great distances has been the subject of much research, some deft experimentation and no little speculation. The mechanics are now to some extent understood, and have been described elsewhere in some detail. Suffice it to say here that there are few sounds so evocative as the trumpeting and clanging of the migrating cranes and geese as they fly high across the Indian sky. The passage of cranes has been described by Basil-Edwardes as 'an impressive sight':

> The observer...will hear one morning a loud clanging call and looking towards the sound will see in the distant sky a vast tangled skein of birds. As it approaches it resolves itself into an immense concourse of cranes flying at a tremendous height. The stream of birds travels across the sky like an army. Big flocks, small parties, single birds and chevrons extend as far as the eye can reach, all travelling the same line. Then perhaps the leading flock circles round in a vast swirl, feeling for its direction; the next formations close up to it and again the army moves forward. As they go a single bird trumpets, answered by others.

Perhaps no less of a thrill is to see of a November morning a skein of geese winging in across the Bharatpur marshes from their breeding grounds many thousands of miles to the north. No visitor to Bharatpur can fail to marvel at one of nature's most remarkable phenomena.

# STORKS

*A meditative Painted Stork* (Mycteria leucocephala) *in a lush post-monsoon Eden. These long-legged, omnivorous birds are associated in India with wetland habitats, with local movements depending on water conditions.*

OF THE world's seventeen species of stork, seven have been recorded at Bharatpur and four are commonly to be found there. This number is exceeded only in Africa, where eight species of stork are to be found. All the species at Bharatpur, except the White Stork which is an uncommon visitor from the Middle East and at least in part from Europe, are resident or locally migratory birds.

# The Painted Stork

## (Mycteria leucocephalus)

For the summer or autumn visitor to Bharatpur, the Painted Stork is easily the most noticeable species. Partly this is a question of numbers: some 5,000 nesting pairs, for example, were counted in the Park in 1980 and, at least until the most recent drought, their numbers remained appreciable. As a general rule, the extent of breeding, and hence the size of the following year's breeding population, seems to reflect the strength of the monsoon, a high rate of reproduction being usual in a year when a heavy rainfall has brought with it an abundance of fish. But the Painted Stork is also noticeable on account of its appearance, which can certainly be termed spectacular but at the same time is ungainly and not a little bizarre. The basic effect is of a long-necked, long-legged white bird with black markings and a large, heavy beak which, together with the neck, seems much out of proportion to the whole. Also, not only is the yellow of the beak barely attuned with the orange-red of the head, but both colours positively clash with some delicate pink patches on the lower back. The bird is undoubtedly 'painted', but a good match of colours is rather obtrusively lacking.

Some interesting research has been done in India into the breeding activities of this stork, the annual cycle of which commences during August, soon after the onset of the monsoon. When the birds arrive at their nesting trees, which they occupy year after year and which in Bharatpur are mainly Babul (*Acacia nilotica*), the search begins for suitable niches. These often consist of the remnants of nests left over from previous years. The males mark out and defend territories, while the females each try to attract the attention of a male who is in possession of an acceptable piece of tree-top. If her tentative approaches are well received, both birds set the seal on their union with an elaborate bowing ceremony, following which they start in earnest to consolidate their nest. As in the home life of other species, the male provides and the female arranges, using twigs, branches and water vines, some of which may appear ridiculously long and others impossibly small. When building is complete, each tree consists of a colony of packed nests. These are often of Painted Storks alone, but sometimes they are in company with one or more other breeding species, although the latter then tend on the whole to gravitate to the lower branches. Nests can be as close as a foot apart and the degree of mutual tolerance is remarkable, at least until the arrival of the offspring, when conditions become excessively crowded. The birds continue to add to and repair their nests throughout the breeding season.

It is no accident at all that the breeding season coincides with an abundance of monsoon water in the Bharatpur marshes. This in turn produces an abundance of fish, which also spawn around monsoon time. Each pair of storks produces between two and four eggs, which hatch out over a period of a few days at the end of about a month's incubation. During incubation the pair mount a round-the-clock attendance at the nest, changing guard with a bowing and beak-clattering ritual. This, which has been termed the 'up-down' display, is also a feature of the behaviour of other varieties of stork. Both birds point their beaks upwards, with their gapes wide open, and utter what has been described as a weak hissing scream, rather like the 'fizz' of a bottle of lemonade as it is opened. The head and neck are then bowed downwards and moved from side to side. Between the vocalisations the beaks are snapped audibly several times in rapid succession, but there is no prolonged clattering as in the case of other species. This seems only to take place during copulation or in confrontations with other birds.

Once the eggs are hatched, a feverish activity commences, with the parents having to fetch an inordinate amount of fish for their fast-growing offspring. One calculation puts the amount of fish which a young stork eats in the first two months or so of its life at something approaching thirty kilograms. Another calculation puts the consumption of fish by a colony of a hundred nests at some twenty-four tonnes over the breeding season. Some rather more extensive work by Dr Salim Ali, in the form of a census carried out in October 1942, took as its starting point the reckoning that in an area of about 1.5 square kilometres of the Park there were at that time, at a conservative estimate, between two and three thousand Painted Storks feeding young of various ages: possibly there may have been as many as 4,000. Every tree was crowded out and other varieties of birds, chiefly cormorants and White Ibises, were also present in the nesting colonies. Dr Salim Ali went on to observe that when a fully fed fledgling was handled, its immediate reaction was to disgorge its fish and then to collapse in a heap, doing its best to pretend that it was in the last agonies of death. He was thus able to form an estimate of the amount of fish in each fledgling's latest meal, and it appeared that the normal quantity was some four or five fish, weighing in total between 200 and 300 grams. Assuming two young to a nest (although, as noted above, three was also common and four not unknown), each being fed twice a day, the assumption per

The Painted Stork nests colonially, often in association with other varieties of stork as well as with cormorants and darters. Both sexes participate in nest building, incubation and rearing of offspring.

Painted Stork nestlings are intolerant of the heat of the sun, and so a principal preoccupation of the parents during the nesting season is to shade their young with wings outstretched.

nest per day thus worked out at the order of a kilogram or so, and the total consumption some two to three thousand kilograms. Given that the nesting period of these birds lasts for some thirty to forty days, and assuming very conservatively two thousand kilograms per day for thirty days, the final figure worked out at an awesome minimum of sixty tonnes for this single species alone. And it has to be reckoned that other species, for example the cormorants, are barely less numerous and voracious.

A further preoccupation of the parents during the nesting period is to shade their offspring from the heat of the sun, and they spend hours at this task with wings outstretched. Of the two or three original nestlings, only about one on average is successfully raised. Predation and accidents account for some fatalities, but more often the younger chicks simply have difficulty in competing for food with their older siblings. Unusually, the Painted Stork does not feed food into its offspring's gullets, nor do the offspring take it from their parents' throats. The parent, having returned to the nest and paused a while, possibly for a measure of predigestion, merely disgorges its catch in a slimy heap on the floor of the nest, leaving the nestlings to compete for it as best they can. The weaker thus soon go to the wall.

The chicks take an appreciable time to grow up and fly. Their plumage passes through a series of changes and for several months they are a rather dirty grey, with none of the colouring of the adult bird. They may take between two and three months before being capable of flight, and are still to be seen for several weeks thereafter before they finally leave. It is not until about April that the colonies are once again fully deserted and the birds disperse until the cycle resumes with the onset of the following monsoon.

The Painted Stork is a voiceless bird, apart from the 'fizz' described above and what has been charitably described as the occasional grunt or moan. To express anything approaching a respectable range of emotion, the adult bird has to rely on beak clattering and display gestures. The young birds, however, have no such physical restriction and manage without difficulty to produce a harsh cry, the motivation for which, namely hunger, is not difficult to discern. But they gradually lose their vocal abilities and are condemned to a lifelong dumbness by the time they are eighteen months old.

The Painted Stork is also a great soarer, and scores can often be seen at Bharatpur circling upwards in the midday thermals, sometimes in company with pelicans or vultures. They fish by stalking around in shallow water with partly open mandibles, often in flocks, stirring the mud with their feet and occasionally flicking a wing to startle a fish into movement. It seems as if they fish by touch rather than by sight.

# The Open-bill Stork

## (Anastomus oscitans)

The only other stork which nests gregariously at Bharatpur is the Open-bill, so called because its mandibles are arched, leaving an open gap between them. The purpose of this odd shape has not been credibly explained, although one theory is that it has something to do with the bird's method of dealing with the fresh-water snail (*Pila globosa*) which is one of its favourite foods. Opponents of this theory have observed, however, that the bird appears to use the tip of its lower beak to prise open these snails and extract the body content, although they have had in turn to admit that the process of splitting open shells and extracting the contents is so dexterous and rapid as to have prevented it from being reliably observed. The fact that it more often than not happens under water does not exactly assist observation. A somewhat odder theory is that the gap is gradually opened as the bird crushes the shells of the molluscs on which it feeds; but nobody has explained why, if this is so, this peculiarity is confined to this species of bird alone. A more likely explanation is that the bill is simply a quirk of nature, its shape serving no particularly useful purpose. But a curious aspect is that the bill does warp with age, the young birds having normal beaks so long as they are in the nest.

The Open-bill is a small stork, an immaculate white with a blackish mantle at the commencement of the breeding season, and with bright, deep-pink legs. However the white changes to a dull grey soon after the eggs are laid, apparently due to an alteration in the colouring of the feathers rather than a moult, and the legs turn to a duller pink. Perhaps, having successfully won a mate, it sees no further need to keep up appearances, or possibly the cares of parenthood have a dimming effect. At any rate, while nesting by the side of the Painted Stork, the Open-bill seems rather drab, although its habits and rituals are very similar. It too nests at Bharatpur in large numbers, although it is by no means as numerous as the Painted species and its breeding season is earlier and shorter. When observed during the 1966 season, for example, some birds started to lay early in August and many had completed laying by the third week of that month. In the following year, however, both the monsoon flooding and the egg-laying began some ten days later, which suggests that the timing of breeding may be regulated by the availability of the fresh-water snail, which in turn is brought out of aestivation by the monsoon.

An interesting habit of the bird is that it can be seen intermittently regurgitating a quantity of water over its eggs, perhaps in order to keep them cool or possibly to regulate the humidity in their

Overleaf: *The Open-bill Stork* (Anastomus oscitans) *is the smallest and commonest of storks with social habits very similar to those of its Painted relative. It is a resident bird found around inland waters and tidal mud flats, where it feeds chiefly on molluscs, and also on frogs, crabs and other small marsh creatures.*

Top: *The White-necked Stork*
(Ciconia episcopus), *a silent
and solitary bird, is a resident
of the sub-continent though
sparsely distributed. It feeds
on frogs, reptiles, molluscs
and large insects, chiefly from
the bank.*

Bottom: *The Black-necked
Stork* (Ephippiorhynchus
asiaticus) *is also a solitary
bird. It has an interesting
greeting ceremony which
features beak-clattering,
touching of wing-tips and
fanning of wings.*

immediate neighbourhood. The Open-bill displays in the 'up-down' fashion in a manner very similar to that of the Painted Stork although the neck is more strongly arched and the vocalisation is a rather loud, repeated, low-pitched honking sound. No clattering takes place during the greeting display, although during copulation the male raps his beak rapidly back and forth against that of the female. Also like the Painted Stork, the Open-bill is a great soarer, and has the giddy habit of parachuting and side-slipping down to earth with wings half pulled in and legs outstretched, at a speed which appears almost unmanageable.

Another curious feature, as Dr Salim Ali has noted, is that the Open-bill has the not infrequent habit of crashing into lighthouses in central and southern India during August and September, at times when the nights have been dark and the visibility poor. Were it not for this phenomenon, the bird would have been looked upon as a somewhat idle local migrant, but it seems as if the young birds may 'go walk-about' for a while after they have left their nests. One young bird ringed at Bharatpur was found five hundred miles to the east only a few months later. Having seen something of the world, they no doubt return home and become dutiful parents ever after.

# The Black-necked Stork

## (Ephippiorhynchus asiaticus)

This is another rather bizarre and ungainly stork which, however, unlike the two previous species, is shy and solitary by nature and is to be seen at Bharatpur generally in ones or twos. In reality it is not black-necked at all, as the so-called black areas, the head, neck and tail, are brilliantly glossed with purple, metallic bluish-green and coppery-brown. The back and underparts are white, while a black beak and coral-red legs complete a striking picture. Nevertheless, like the Painted Stork, this bird also seems oddly put together, with its massive bill and long legs out of proportion to its relatively truncated body.

When one sees this stork at Bharatpur, it is generally stalking along on dry land or wading in the shallows; often it kneels to rest on its tarsi, when its anatomy appears oddly back to front, at least to one of an anthropomorphic cast of mind, since of course its lower legs point forwards. At other times it wades deep into the marshes, where its great length of leg and beak gives it an extensive range. It feeds mostly on fish, crabs, reptiles and molluscs.

Several pairs of Black-necked Storks nest at Bharatpur, some in or on the verges of the marshland and others in the dry areas. A year or two ago, one pair was unwise enough to start nesting in a tree on the edge of Mound Plantation, in close proximity to the Fishing Eagles' nest there: when the eagles arrived they took strong exception to the companionship and harassed the storks until the latter were compelled to start a fresh construction at a more respectful distance. The nests of the Black-necked Stork are solitary and massive, often some six feet across and three to four feet deep, set in the crowns of Peepul or Kadam trees. Constructed externally of small branches and sticks, they are lined internally with rushes, grass or similar material, and sometimes there is a parapet of mud. Egg-laying seems to start in September or October, and the breeding season continues until January. Three to five eggs are normally laid. Often the nest is reused year after year.

Relatively speaking, these storks are undemonstrative on the nest. Their greeting display is a singular one, consisting of the two birds facing each other with bills held vertically downwards, fluttering their outstretched wings until the tips brush together. Sometimes this is accompanied by a clattering of beaks, while on other occasions the 'up-down' display has also been seen. Unusually, the sex of these birds can be determined with ease, the male having a dark brown iris, whereas the female's is lemon yellow. This stork too is fond of soaring, particularly when thermals form in the heat of the day. With its black head and neck and a broad black stripe running down the centre of each wing contrasting with the pure white of the rest of the plumage, its appearance in flight is striking and unmistakable.

# The White-necked Stork

## (Ciconia episcopus)

This, unlike the Black-necked Stork, is a quite well-put-together, even elegant, bird. For one thing, its beak is not disproportionately long or heavy, while for another its white neck and tail coverts provide an agreeable contrast to the crown and body, which are black glossed with brown and green. Like the Black-necked Stork, however, it is a solitary bird and is to be seen at Bharatpur mainly in ones and twos, and very occasionally in small parties. It is not a particularly active bird, although, like other storks, it enjoys soaring: when it is not quietly feeding it is mostly to be seen roosting in trees or standing around as if in meditation. It is perhaps this rather solemn life-style, as well as the black 'cap' on its head, which prompted the classifier to give it its Latin name 'episcopus' – 'like a bishop'.

It too is an exclusively solitary nester and, apart from the occasional bill clapping, does not indulge much in social display. The nest is a substantial, untidy structure of branches and twigs with a lining of grass or feathers, built high in a tree but not necessarily near water. In fact it takes most of its prey on dry land or mud banks, seldom wading or immersing its bill. Three eggs are normally laid.

Overleaf: *In the haven of marsh and woodland provided by Bharatpur, a lone Black-necked Stork forages peacefully amid an assortment of other water-birds.*

# CORMORANTS
# & DARTERS

ALTHOUGH several of the nesting colonies at Bharatpur are the
exclusive or near-exclusive preserve of the Painted Stork, as has
been noted, it is more usual to find groups of trees shared between
the storks and a variety of other bids. In some places, indeed, the
storks are absent or few in number and a mix of other species takes
over. Of these, the cormorants are perhaps the most numerous, and
many trees contain few or no other types of bird. Around the Park,
both in the nesting season and at other times, cormorants and
darters seem also to enjoy sitting in groups on the branches of
leafless trees, sometimes spreading their wings out to dry and
sometimes just contemplating the environment. Individuals are
likewise frequently seen sitting bolt upright on a tree stump or
similar solitary perch, again often drying their wings. They hunt both
singly, when they show to perfection their remarkable skills at
swimming and diving, and in flocks, which often progress across a
marsh in a wide arc, driving the fish before them. They are strong
fliers, although they have to make long and laborious efforts to flap
their way off the water and become airborne. One of the sights of
Bharatpur at the height of the breeding season is the immense flights
of cormorants returning to their nests or roosts of an evening. At
other times of the year the cormorants seem largely to disperse away
from the Park, although there are always a small number present.
They are assumed to migrate only locally for the most part, but a
small number of recoveries of ringed Common Cormorants show
that there is some pattern of long-distance migration between India
and Khazakhstan.

Of the three species of cormorant which breed at Bharatpur, the
largest in size is the Common Cormorant ( *Phalacrocorax carbo*).
This is the glossy black cormorant which frequents the sea coasts of
Britain and is found across North America, mainland Europe, North
Africa, Asia and Australasia. It can be readily identified by its size, by
its yellow bill and throat pouch, and by its white throat and cheeks.
During the breeding season it also develops white thigh patches,
which feature in courtship displays. These, which seem usually to
take place at the nest, consist of rapid wing and head raising and
lowering on the part of the male, timed so that the white throat and

Opposite: *The Large
Cormorant* (Phalacrocorax
carbo) *is a resident and
locally migratory bird, found
in the neighbourhood of
inland waters, including
Himalayan lakes and rivers.
Both the Large and the Small
Cormorant are known as
Pan-kauwa, 'water crows',
and viewed as competitors by
fishermen because of their
voracious appetite for fish.*

*The Little Cormorant
(Phalacrocorax niger) is a
resident bird, generally
solitary but seen at places like
Bharatpur in great flocks,
when water conditions
favour an abundance of fish.
Like the Darter, a close
relative, its plumage is
permeable to water; both
these birds are frequently seen
perched on rocks or branches
with wings hung out to dry
like washing.*

thigh patches are displayed in quick alternation. For some reason as yet unexplained, the Common Cormorant was at one time having reproduction problems at Bharatpur, the great majority of the eggs laid turning out to be infertile. After a few years, however, breeding again seemed to occur normally.

At the other end of the scale is the Little Cormorant (*Phalacrocorax niger*), which is also an overall black in colour. However, it sports a small white throat patch during the breeding season, while a few silky white feathers grow on the sides of the head and neck. In contrast to the Common Cormorant, the numbers of the Little Cormorant at Bharatpur are currently showing a steady increase. Intermediate between the Common and Little Cormorants is the Indian Shag (*Phalacrocorax fuscicollis*) which is not easy to distinguish outside the breeding season, when it grows white feather tufts behind the eyes.

A rather more elegant and attractive bird than any of the cormorants is the Indian Darter (*Anhinga rufa melanogaster*). This bird's predominant colouring is also black, but this is relieved by silvery streaks on the back and by a brown head and neck with a white throat and chin. Its head and neck are long, slender and sinuous, characteristics which have earned it the name of 'Snake Bird'—a description which seems particularly apt when it is seen swimming in its customary fashion, with its body wholly submerged

and only its head and neck turning and swaying above the surface. It is interesting to compare its method of fishing with that of the cormorant and to note the variations in physiognomy which match the differences in style between the two. First of all, the darter has a long, spear-like beak whereas the cormorant has a shorter, broader beak with a terminal hook. The darter thus, more often than not, impales its prey instead of gripping it, and this operation is assisted by a hinge mechanism in the neck which enables the bird to deliver a powerful thrust of the beak from an S-shaped position. It is a common sight to see a darter surface with an impaled fish, which it then throws up and swallows head first. Furthermore, whereas the cormorant uses its strongly muscled body and legs to pursue and catch fish, the darter, which is a weaker swimmer, is able to take advantage of its relative lack of buoyancy to swim slowly beneath the surface and steal up on its prey, rather in the manner of a diver with a spear-gun. Two other characteristics of the darter are a reluctance to take off from the water—wherever possible, having more versatile legs than the cormorant, it prefers to paddle ashore; and its habit, when alarmed, of flopping off a tree straight into the water, crashing through the intervening foliage if necessary, and surfacing when a safe distance away. A darter will usually dive to escape danger, and will only fly when it has a clear take-off path and sufficient height not to hit the surface before it can gather flying speed and climb away.

*The Darter or Snake-bird* (Anhinga rufa), *another resident fish-eating bird that favours inland waters, owes its names to its distinctive method of harpooning fish and to the sinuous movements of its snorkel-like head and neck as it swims.*

# SPOONBILLS & IBISES

A LTHOUGH IT is not altogether obvious at first sight, the Spoonbill (*Platalea leucorodia*) and the ibises are closely related, to the extent, indeed, that hybrids between the two have been produced in captivity. The relationship is perhaps at its clearest when the two are seen in flight, there being a marked similarity in the shape and posture of the outstretched head and neck, as well as in the silhouette of the wings and the long legs stretched out behind a wedge-shaped tail. Very similar also is the manner of flying, with measured wing flaps alternating with short glides. Where the two most obviously differ is in the shape of the bill, that of the ibises being slender and downcurved, very like that of the curlew, and employed in an identical manner for probing for food in mud and shallow water. As its name suggests, the Spoonbill on the other hand has a long, spatulate bill which is used uniquely for detecting floating prey in shallow water. The modus operandi is to sweep it, slightly opened, from side to side and to snap it shut on any edible object which is touched. Often a number of these birds fish collectively, advancing across a shallow marsh in close order and sweeping it systematically. Such periods of intense activity seem to alternate with periods of meditative calm, and small flocks of Spoonbills are as often as not to be seen at Bharatpur grouped quietly around the marshes.

Both the Spoonbill and the White Ibis (*Threskiornis melanocephala*) are found in appreciable numbers in the Bharatpur nesting colonies, cheek by jowl with one another and the rest of the nesting birds. The Spoonbill is of the slightly larger Asian race (*Pl. l. major*), which is found in Egypt and through Central and southern Asia to China and Japan. It has been suggested that those which are found in the Indian sub-continent are not all breeding residents, but that some at least migrate from the Caspian Sea area (as proved by ring recoveries) and perhaps elsewhere. They are snow-white birds with, in adulthood, a yellowish-buff patch on the foreneck, while they also sport a yellow patch of bare skin at the throat, fringed with red. The flat 'spoon' at the tip of the black bill is also tinged with yellow. The Spoonbill is at its most spectacular during the breeding season, when it develops a long, drooping nuchal crest.

Opposite: *Spoonbills* (Platalea leucorodia) *fighting. These gregarious and sociable birds are abundant in Bharatpur in winter.*

37

Top: *Spoonbills have a strong
and level flight, and are less
prone than ibises to soaring
and gliding for sheer
enjoyment. But both groups
fly with legs trailing behind
and neck extended, like
storks.*

Bottom: *The Oriental White
Ibis* (Threskiornis aethiopica) *was revered in Ancient Egypt
(where it is now extinct) as a
reincarnation of the god
Thoth, and figures
prominently in hieroglyphs
and tomb paintings. It eats
fish, frogs and molluscs but
also carrion and—
deplorably—flamingo eggs.*

The White Ibis is much less striking in appearance, lacking as it does not only the buff and yellow colourings but also the extraordinary bill. Its plumage is white beneath a naked—and rather ugly—black head and neck, although in the breeding season the primary feathers assume a brownish colour and patches of grey develop along the scapulars, while a tuft of long plumes also appears at the base of the neck. Like the majority of the birds at Bharatpur, both the Spoonbill and the White Ibis lack a true vocal apparatus, although they do manage to produce a certain amount of low key grunting, particularly during the breeding season. The White Ibis tends to breed earlier than the Spoonbill, laying a clutch of two to four eggs in June-August, while the latter lays a clutch of four eggs and has a breeding season which extends between July and November.

Two other ibises, the Black Ibis (*Pseudibis papillosa*) and Glossy Ibis (*Plegadis falcinellus*), are also found at Bharatpur, although in much smaller numbers. The Black Ibis, which is slightly smaller than the White Ibis, is a bird of an overall dark olive brown colour with wings of black tinged with purple-green. The head and face are black, and are crowned by a bizarre patch of red warts, a feature which accounts not only for the Latin name but also for the species' alternative name of Warty-headed Ibis. A final distinguishing mark is a prominent white patch on the coverts. Nests are normally built high in a tree, quite separately or in very small groups, and not necessarily near water, since, on the whole, the Black Ibis seems to prefer open country to marshland. Its range covers not only the Indian sub-continent, where it is widely resident, but also parts of Burma and South-East Asia. Its two- or three-note screaming cry rather resembles that of a bird of prey.

Smaller again is the Glossy Ibis, which also breeds widely across India. In the breeding season its plumage is a dark reddish-brown, with wings and tail attractively glossed in purple and green. Outside the breeding season it is rather duller overall, but develops streaks of pale feathers on the head and neck. It shares nesting sites with the White Ibis and is said to nest colonially, but has not been seen doing so at Bharatpur, where it is an occasional visitor, either singly or in small groups. Unlike the other two species, it is highly cosmopolitan, and is found from south-eastern Europe through parts of Africa and the Middle East to South Asia and Australasia, as well as in eastern North America. Like other ibises, which have from time immemorial befriended the farmer through their consumption of insect pests, particularly in irrigated areas, the range and numbers of the Glossy Ibis have been much reduced with the disappearance of wetlands and the use of pesticides.

# HERONS
# & EGRETS

T O COMPLETE the tally of the colonial nesting birds at Bharatpur,
it remains to give some account of the large numbers of egrets
and the smaller numbers of herons which are also found among
them. Prominent among the herons, in terms of both numbers and
visibility, is the Common Heron (*Ardea cinerea*), one of the Old
World's most familiar birds and found at Bharatpur in its Eastern
form, *Ardea c. rectirostris*. There are in fact three races of Common
Heron, each recognisably distinct: in the West the race is *Ardea c.
cinerea*, which occasionally reaches the north-west of the Indian
sub-continent as a migrant, while the resident race of the
sub-continent, and also of Burma, is *Ardea c. rectirostris*. In the Far
East, this is superceded by *Ardea c. jouyi*, the species becoming
progressively lighter in colour the further east it occurs.

This is by no means the only species which varies geographically
in this manner. The Common Crane (*Grus grus*), for example, and
the Greylag Goose (*Anser anser*) are each also found in Western and
Eastern forms. The interesting feature is that in none of these species
is there a hard and fast boundary between the races: rather there is a
'cline' or progressive transition, with numbers of 'intermediates'
which are clearly the result of interbreeding. The inference is that the
races have at some stage been wholly separated, to the extent that
they have developed distinct characteristics, but not to the extent that
interbreeding has ceased to be possible. An attractive, if unproveable,
theory is that the separations took place during a former Ice Age,
which effectively divided each species for a substantial period of
time, but that interbreeding recommenced once the ice had receded.

At Bharatpur, there are no distinct 'heronries' as such, and the
Common Heron is found nesting in smallish numbers in company
with other species. However it remains a solitary hunter, its preferred
haunt being shallow water at the base of a tree, with which one
imagines it blends well when viewed from the perspective of an
approaching fish. Bharatpur herons are among the shyer species and
are prompt to depart with a melancholy croak as soon as they are
approached.

A little smaller, fewer in numbers and even more retiring by nature
is the Eastern Purple Heron (*Ardea purpurea manilensis*). While the

Opposite: *The Grey Heron*
(Ardea cinerea) *is one of the
commonest and best known
of herons of the Old World.
These attractive, long-legged
waders are gregarious and
nest colonially in tree-tops.*

Top: *The Intermediate Egret* (Egretta intermedia) *is difficult to distinguish outside of the breeding season from the Eastern Large Egret, but it is more commonly seen, and is a more gregarious bird.*

Opposite: *The Great White Egret* (Egretta alba) *is a rare winter straggler from its breeding grounds in Europe. It is usually solitary, and seldom seen in groups of more than two or three.*

Common Heron's colourings of black, white and grey are no doubt adequately disruptive to facilitate its static method of fishing, they are, as camouflage, nothing when compared with the attractive colourings of the Purple Heron, a crepuscular bird which is often extremely hard to distinguish against the background of reeds and other vegetation in which it tends to lurk by day. On the upper parts, the predominant colour is a purplish-blue, while the underparts are chestnut and black. The crown and crest are black, the head and neck chestnut striped boldly with black, the throat and foreneck white, and the upper breast covered with long white plumes streaked with black and chestnut. The combination is not only most attractive, but also provides a highly effective concealment, particularly since the bird's frequent response to any alarm is to freeze.

Also crepuscular in habit but of a wholly contrasting shape is the Night Heron (*Nycticorax nycticorax*), a thick-set, short-legged heron with a commensurately short, thick bill. It is largely grey above, but with a glossy black crown and back, while the underparts are white, and two long white plumes form an elegant crest. At Bharatpur, a number of these herons are in the habit of roosting in the trees at the water's edge near the Keoladeo temple. Here they spend their days in their typically hunched posture, partly concealed among the foliage and staring at the world outside with an unwavering red eye. If disturbed, they explode into flight and, as Dr Salim Ali has put it,

'mill about like a rabble of flying foxes'. As evening approaches, they fly out in ones or twos to their various fishing grounds, where they prefer to search actively for their food rather than stand and wait for it in the manner of the Common and Purple Herons.

Similar to the Night Heron in shape is the Pond Heron or Paddy Bird (*Ardeola grayii*), one of the commonest birds of the Indian countryside: there can hardly be a patch of water without its Paddy Bird in residence, slowly and carefully stalking its prey or standing concealed in the vegetation. With an overall colouring on the upper parts of various shades of brown streaked with buff, it is an extremely well camouflaged bird when at rest and is very hard to see when not in the open. However, when it flies there is a flash of snow-white wings, and there departing with slow flaps is a totally transfigured bird. There is also something of a transfiguration during the breeding season, when the head and neck lighten and the back darkens to a deep maroon, while long white plumes develop on the back and breast and a handsome white or buff crest appears on the head.

Of the four varieties of egret which haunt the Bharatpur marshes, the most spectacular but at the same time the least numerous is the Eastern Large Egret (*Egretta alba modesta*), a tall, slender, snow-white bird, solitary by nature like the Common Heron and indeed very similar to it both in feeding habits and in behaviour generally. Outside the breeding season it has a yellow bill and black legs, but in the breeding season the bill turns black (although with some residual yellow at the base), the eye-patch becomes green and the upper parts of the legs yellow. Also in the breeding season this egret develops long, lacy plumes from the scapulars to beyond the tail which, when erected and spread, form a magnificent spray which has been graphically described as a 'halo of mist'.

Slightly smaller and hard to distinguish from the Large Egret outside the breeding season is the Smaller or Median Egret (*Egretta intermedia*): in the breeding season it has long plumes on the breast as well as on the back. This is both a more common and more gregarious bird than the Large Egret, but less common than the Little Egret (*Egretta garzetta*), which is smaller still and very similar to the two other species. Its distinguishing marks are a black bill at all seasons and yellow feet. In the breeding season it not only grows ornamental plumes on the breast and back, but also a pair of long narrow plumes which droop from the head. It is this bird which earlier in this century was slaughtered in appreciable numbers in India and elsewhere for the aigrettes which formed a much sought-after item of female fashion. It was also caught, bred and 'farmed' in captivity by the *mirbahars*, the inland fishermen of the province of Sind. Some intriguing descriptions of the methods used were published at the time, from which it appears that the egrets were treated quite humanely, if only because they were valuable birds. They were confined in enclosures of woven reeds and provided with fish, water and nesting materials. They duly paired off, marked out territories and bred in a normal manner. The chicks were subsequently removed as soon as they could be hand-reared, and this induced the parents to resume breeding, with plumage again developing to match, often as frequently as four or five times in a year. It seems that it was not until the 1930s that the fashion finally changed and put the farms out of business. Even while they had flourished they had had to rely on middlemen being able to smuggle the plumes out of India, since the authorities took the view that an export ban was essential in order to reduce slaughter in the wild. It is said that at one time the aigrettes were worth not far short of their weight in silver.

The other egret found at Bharatpur, and perhaps the most numerous of all, is the Cattle Egret (*Bubulcus ibis coromandus*). This again is a snow-white bird, differing from the Little Egret in having a yellow bill and black feet. Apart from its smaller size it is not readily distinguishable from the two larger egrets outside the breeding season. In that season it develops a golden-buff plumage on the head, neck and back which is both striking and unmistakable. As its name implies, it is to be found more often than not in the company of cattle, frequently riding on their backs and feeding off insects which they harbour or which they disturb as they graze. It was, for example, a common partner of the buffaloes which used to frequent the Park. It is gregarious not only when nesting but also often when feeding, and large flocks can be seen from time to time fishing together across the marshes. It is particularly intriguing to watch these and other egrets feeding their offspring on the nest. They indeed regurgitate fish, as do many of the other nesting species, but the young seem able to induce their parents to do so only by gripping their beaks with their own and almost wrestling the fish out of them. Why there should be a need for this seemingly highly uncomfortable, if not painful, treatment of the parent birds is an unexplained mystery.

# CRANES

One of the foremost attractions of Bharatpur is its cranes, and observers during the winter months can in normal years spot at least four species, three of them migrants. The Sarus Crane (Grus antigone), *seen here in the fading evening light, is a common resident and revered all over the country as a symbol of marital fidelity.*

FOR ME, as for many people, there is something very special about cranes. Partly it is their quite exceptional beauty and elegance; partly it is the reverence they often inspire—in Japan, for example, they are a symbol of longevity, while among Buddhists they are held in religious awe. In India, no villager would dare to harm the Sarus Crane for fear of ill-luck. Partly also there is something primeval about the crane; while it is not among the oldest groups of birds, it has survived on this earth for very many years—some 40 million, to judge from the fossil record, which stretches from the Eocene. It is therefore all the more distressing that in our generation it is perhaps, of all avian families, the one most in need of protection and conservation, several of its species being on the verge of extinction. Not least, there is the uniqueness of its habits, its bizarre dances and trumpeting, and the sight and sound of it while migrating, which makes it so unforgettable. Of the world's fourteen species of crane, four are to be found at Bharatpur, three of them migratory and one, the Sarus Crane, resident.

# The Sarus Crane

## (Grus antigone)

While the peafowl is said to be the national bird of India, a no less natural choice would be the Sarus Crane. This huge grey bird, standing the height of a man and topped by a red head and face, is a common sight across the Indian countryside, being resident over most of the north of the sub-continent. It is often to be found in the vicinity of villages and is held in veneration by the villagers. It can become quite tame and can even be kept as a pet, when it makes an excellent watchman. The awe it inspires perhaps owes something to its uncommon faithfulness to its mate: these cranes pair for life and mutual devotion appears to be strong. They are never seen far apart and they fly closely together, one behind the other; and Indians will tell you that if one is killed, the survivor will die of a broken heart. This was commented upon by the Mughal emperor Jehangir, who was a keen and astute naturalist and sportsman. Among his exhaustive notes on the Sarus Crane, which he held in special regard, are references to the pining and deaths of birds whose mates had been killed.

Large numbers of Sarus Cranes congregate at Bharatpur in March or April, but there are some to be seen at any time of the year. Over 300 were, for instance, counted there in February 1969, although numbers have certainly decreased in the last decade, due very probably to the disturbance and even destruction of their nests by wading buffaloes. These congregations, and similar congregations elsewhere, are something of a mystery. They are never permanent,

but seem to be more of what Dr Salim Ali has called a 'gathering of the clans'. The birds display and trumpet, with pairs and groups joining in and breaking away from time to time.

The trumpeting of these birds, which, as with most cranes, is engineered by a peculiar coiling of the wind pipe, is loud and far-carrying, and there is no possibility of being in ignorance of the presence of a pair of Sarus Cranes in the vicinity. The unearthly noise which they make seems to be not merely their means of keeping in touch or warning each other of danger, or even a greeting (for example when changing incubation duty at the nest), although it is probably all of these at various times. It appears also to be a sign of affection, the call of one bird being invariably answered by the other until a raucous duet is set up. While calling, both birds stretch their necks skywards, but while the female holds her wings closely against her sides, the male raises his secondaries in an arch above his back,

*A pair of Sarus Cranes conducting their spectacular nuptial dance consisting of elaborate leaps, bows, capers and trumpeting calls.*

49

while holding the primaries stiffly downwards, rather in the manner of a turkey cock. The whole performance is thus as curious in appearance as it is assaulting to the ears.

The Sarus Crane's courtship display is remarkable, and no description can better that of Dr Salim Ali:

> Courtship display during the breeding season is exceedingly animated, spectacular and also somewhat ludicrous; it is mutually performed like the duetting, though the female is somewhat less active. The male usually gives the cue by suddenly flicking his wings half open, bowing, giving a little leap, throwing up his head and trumpeting loudly. This invitation to dance is promptly taken up by the female. For the next two or three minutes the two birds go through a bout of vigorous courtseying, capering and wildly leaping at, around, and away from each other as if completely demented, duetting all the time. In the midst of all this the female sometimes crouches invitingly, legs partly folded, and copulation takes place. More often, however, the dance dies down as it began, the birds presently resuming their normal activities.

The Sarus generally builds its nest either in shallow water or on a patch of dry land in the midst of farmland, the structure being formed of a large heap of reeds and rushes. Two eggs are normally laid immediately after the monsoon and both parents share the incubation, although guard duties are more often the responsibility of the male. As the Emperor Jehangir also observed, the eggs are laid about two days apart and the incubation period is some four to five weeks. I have myself seen pairs with two well-grown young at Bharatpur, but it is more common for only one chick to reach maturity. Dr Salim Ali has given a fascinating account of an encounter with two cranes and two chicks which provides evidence of their survival tactics. From the commencement of his approach, the parents were on the alert and began to lead the chicks away. Then one of the parents uttered a series of short staccato calls, a subdued 'kor-r-r', at which point the chicks simply vanished. The male then employed diversionary tactics: in a half-crouched position as if furtively slinking away, he described a semicircle backwards and forwards about twenty yards distant. At one point he waded knee-deep into a puddle, where he spread out and drooped his wings, dipped forwards until his breast and underparts were touching the water and, in Dr Salim Ali's words, 'simulated dire distress'. The male employed variations of this distress display for some ten minutes, accompanied by agitated trumpetings in which he was joined by the female, who had retreated some fifty yards. At other times he advanced to within about ten yards, trumpeting loudly and threateningly, and also repeated the staccato 'kor-r-r' call at intervals.

Meanwhile Dr Salim Ali had been trying to find the chicks. This took a long time and one was never found. The other was nearly trodden on as it was lying doggo among longish grass in a puddle, partly submerged, with only the top of the back and the head to the eyes showing above the water. Its beak was fully stretched in front and resting on the grass at a slight upward angle. It was completely motionless, and remained so for over half an hour while its sibling was being searched for, even when approached to within a foot.

The imprinting of this behaviour by Sarus Cranes was observed by Dr Salim Ali on another occasion, after he had watched the hatching of one of a clutch of two eggs. When alarmed, the sitting parent got up hastily and was about to move from the nest when the chick began to cheep loudly. The parent made the staccato 'korr-r-r' noise, but the chick paid no attention and continued to shuffle and cheep. The parent then repeated the 'korr-r-r' and at the same time gave the chick a gentle peck. At that the chick froze immediately and remained inert for some five minutes, until the parent uttered another distinct note of similar pattern which clearly signified the all-clear.

# The Siberian White Crane

## (Grus leucogeranus)

This crane is the cynosure of Bharatpur—a large, elegant, snow-white bird, one of the glories of the natural world but now rare and listed as a threatened species. At rest, its brick-red face and legs contrast sharply with its white plumage, while black wing quills become visible in flight, a feature which has prompted comparison with the Snow Goose. Among the Chinese, the bird is appropriately known as 'the crane with the black sleeves'.

The Siberian Crane seems in the past to have bred widely across Siberia and flocks of up to 300 birds were at one time to be seen on migration. Accidental migration to Sweden and Japan has been recorded, and regular migration to Japan is noted in old Japanese literature. However its breeding grounds appear now to be confined to north-eastern Yakutia, between the Yana and Kelyne rivers, and to the lower reaches of the Ob river. Until very recently, great uncertainty existed about the numbers and wintering areas of the Eastern population, from Yakutia; and, with the numbers at Bharatpur much depleted, the estimate in the 1980-1 World Wildlife Handbook was that the global population of Siberian Cranes probably amounted to no more than 275. A drastic—and exciting—revision was however made a few years ago when some 1,300 birds were found wintering on the Poyang lakes not far from Nanchang in the Yangstse valley of China. A Russian aerial survey of

*A Siberian Crane wading and probing for aquatic plants in the marshes. Normally they feed in pairs, pausing at intervals to survey their surroundings for any sign of danger.*

the Eastern breeding grounds, conducted in 1960, suggested that breeding pairs were distributed on an average at a density of some twenty-five in an area of some 100 square kilometres. On the basis that the whole breeding grounds covered some two thousand five hundred to three thousand square kilometres, the estimate arrived at was that there may have been a total there of some five hundred to seven hundred breeding pairs. If so, the Eastern population has succeeded in staying remarkably stable over the past quarter of a century. The wintering grounds of the Eastern population are to some degree threatened by the proximity and activities of the local rural Chinese, but the Government in Beijing are well aware of the dangers and are taking active conservation measures. Happily, therefore, and in contrast to fears expressed only recently, the survival of the Siberian Crane, at least from a global point of view, seems fairly well assured.

So far as the Western population, from the Ob river, is concerned, it seems that in the past the Siberian Crane wintered as far west as the Caspian Sea coast and Asia Minor, as well as in various locations in Iran and India. In India, reports suggest that these cranes were to be found at one time at Najafgarh just outside Delhi (a swamp which has now been drained), at Jainagar in Bihar in eastern India, near Nagpur in central India and as far south as Kolleru Lake in Andhra Pradesh. Each year one of the staff at Bharatpur has been in the

practice of taking a look at Pyagpur Lake in Uttar Pradesh, not far
from Agra, where these birds also once wintered, but none have
been there for some years. Outside India, Siberian Cranes have been
seen within the past decade in Kazakhstan and Astrakhan, and a very
small group was discovered in 1978 at Feredoonkenar in the
south-eastern Caspian coastlands of Iran. Fifty-six were also sighted
in 1977 at the Ab-i-Istada, a large lake in eastern Afghanistan some
70 kilometres from Ghazni on the road between Kabul and Kandahar.
However, some uncertainty exists both about their status
there—whether they were resident during the winter or merely on
migration—as well as about the effect on them of the subsequent
Afghan hostilities. They are, unfortunately, good eating, and some
carcasses were reported as having been seen a few years ago in the
Kabul meat bazaar, an observation which bears out suggestions that
no control exists at all over the shooting of game in that country.

So far as Bharatpur is concerned, records show that it was used
regularly by Siberian Cranes until about 1880 when they were no
doubt driven away by the Maharaja's shooting parties; and it is
remarkable that they returned after a gap of some eighty years, once
the shooting had come to a stop. It seems that after three birds had
arrived in 1960, numbers increased rapidly until some 200 were
counted in the winter of 1964-5. In 1967-8, however, only about 100
were present, including 15 pairs each with one young; and 120 were

*A pair of Siberian Cranes
courting, a fascinating ritual
involving movements of the
head and wings which mount
in tempo as the birds'
excitement increases. Like
their Sarus cousins, Siberian
Cranes usually pair for life.*

counted in January 1969. Early in February of that year 86 were counted in one day, including 50 which were clearly paired, six of the pairs having young.

In the 1970s, it seems that 60 or more of these cranes were counted in Bharatpur in most years, but that the drought of 1979-80, when the cranes flew in as usual but left—no one knows whither—within a day or two, gave rise to a serious depletion in numbers. In January 1982 there were 38, a figure which marked a slight increase on the previous year. They included six young, and so it is possible to hope that the population is now stable at what is nevertheless a precariously small number. In 1982-3, there were 33, of which eight were young.

The dangers by which these birds are still threatened as they migrate across Afghanistan will no doubt persist, as will the pressures both on their breeding grounds and, for example in the event of another year of drought, at Bharatpur.

Each year the Siberian Cranes fly some 5,500 kilometres in each direction, and in 1952 they were seen migrating across the Himalayas at a height of over 5,000 metres. They are normally sighted in northern Pakistan towards the middle or end of October. Late in November or early December they arrive at Bharatpur, sometimes being seen on the Jamuna river at Delhi on the final stage of their migration. They normally start to return towards the end of March or early April, arriving at their breeding grounds at the end of May or in early June, when a period of extensive thaw normally sets in. They arrive alone, or in pairs or small flocks, and nesting begins immediately, to the accompaniment of pair dancing. The nest is a rough structure about a yard wide and half a yard high, built of grass or reeds. Two eggs are laid, but, as with the Sarus Crane, almost invariably only one chick is raised. Later in the season the birds again collect in small flocks and they begin their return migration in early September.

At Bharatpur, the Siberian Cranes feed almost exclusively within the marshes, and their diet appears to be almost wholly vegetarian. An analysis made some years ago of the contents of the stomach of a Siberian Crane revealed an absence of any form of animal life, but recorded, remarkably, a number of small pebbles, 'enough to fill a wine glass', mostly quartz or green stones ranging in size from a pin's head to a pea. Of four birds whose stomach contents were analysed in Russia in 1960, three were found to have ingested a purely vegetarian diet, but the fourth had also eaten some small mammals. All contained a quantity of gastrolites, one of them weighing as much as 58.5 grams, and ranging in size up to 10 to 12 mm by 6 to 8 mm. One possibility is that these stones were picked up accidentally over a period of time as the birds probed with their long beaks for the shoots, corms and aquatic plants on which they largely feed. However, in his remarkable book, *The Year of the*

*Greylag Goose*, Konrad Lorenz records having observed young goslings pecking in muddy pools on a pathway or road in an attempt to find small stones which would then help to grind down their fibre-rich diet against the tough inner wall of their stomachs. It is conceivable that the stones found inside the stomachs of the Siberian Cranes serve a similar purpose.

To watch a pair of Siberian Cranes feeding is fascinating: every few minutes as they wade and probe for food, one or the other raises its head and calls softly, as if to reassure its mate that no danger threatens. Like the Sarus Crane, pairs mate for life. Their pairing call is less harsh than that of many other cranes and rather more melodious. As they call, they move their heads backwards and forwards and their wings up and down at the same time, this curious rhythm becoming faster the more excited the birds become.

Both in the Soviet Union and at the International Crane Foundation in Wisconsin, more than two dozen of these birds have been hatched successfully from eggs gathered in the wild, the technique apparently being to subject the egg to periods of cooling, in order to simulate the effect of Siberian winds when the parent birds temporarily leave the nest. Much more significantly, after attempts over five or six years, the ICF in 1981 successfully hatched and bred one Siberian Crane in captivity, by means of artificial insemination and incubation. Thus it is possible to hope that the survival of this magnificent bird may now be assured, whatever happens to it in its natural habitat.Fertile eggs are also now being returned to the Soviet Union for placing in the nests of Common Cranes, in the hope that the hatched birds will migrate with this species over a less extensive—and thus less dangerous—range.

Like other migrant cranes, the Siberian Crane was, sadly, once classified as a game bird, and was a victim of the time-honoured pastime of *shikar*. The naturalist Basil-Edwardes, writing in 1928, noted the shyness of the bird and its habit of staying in the centre of marshes, far from any cover from which it could be stalked. An effective means of approaching within gun-shot, according to him, was to use the cover of a domesticated buffalo. Such animals had a rope passing through their nostrils and around their horns, and the technique was to grasp the rope with arm extended horizontally and to bend the body so that the head and shoulders of the hunter were hidden by the shoulders of the animal. Then, as far as possible keeping in water so that the buffalo's belly was touching the surface and the hunter's legs concealed, the pair made their way towards the birds, starting at least a quarter of a mile away with the hunter making the approach look as natural as possible, encouraging the buffalo to dawdle and meander as if it were free and independent. Then, when within range, the hunter let go the rope and fired from beneath the buffalo's neck.

Basil-Edwardes gives a vivid account of what would then happen:

Top: *Cranes are highly
migratory and usually follow
the same route year after
year. The Siberian Cranes
reach Bharatpur in late
November after an awesome
5,500-km journey across the
Himalayas.*

Opposite: *The Demoiselle
Crane* (Anthropoides virgo) *is
one of the smallest of the
cranes, and one of the most
graceful, but it is deemed a
pest by farmers on account of
the considerable damage it
causes to their crops.*

Before your gun is well off, your sporting companion, who has
a marked distrust of Europeans and white faces, and has been
incessantly endeavouring to kick you throughout your whole
promenade, knocks you head over heels and rushes off towards
his dusky owner, bellowing as if he, and not you were the
injured party.

Barely a sufficient punishment, one would have thought, for one so
crass and insensitive as to hunt this quite exceptional bird.

# The Demoiselle Crane

## (Anthropoides virgo)

This delightful crane, which is normally seen at Bharatpur in small
numbers during the winter season, is much smaller than the two
species just described. It is a grey bird with a black face, neck and
breast, with conspicuous soft white ear tufts behind the eyes. The
black feathers of the lower neck fall in long plumes over its breast,
while the tail feathers are also less bunched and more drooping than

those of other cranes. The whole effect is one of grace and elegance. At close quarters a striking feature is its ruby-red eye.

This crane once bred in Rumania and southern Spain, but its main breeding concentrations are now mostly in Central Asia across to Mongolia and, less commonly, the Crimea and Ukraine. It appears also to breed in smaller numbers in Algeria and other parts of North Africa. It migrates southward to Africa in very considerable numbers during the winter, and flocks of up to 20,000 have been seen along the Nile south of Khartoum. In India the Demoiselle Cranes arrive in October in large numbers, spreading across the sub-continent southwards as far as Mysore. Known locally as *Koonj*, they have been keenly hunted, the more so as they are extremely difficult to approach and yet make excellent eating. They often spend the heat of the day soaring or resting, normally close to water, but pay visits to cultivated land in the mornings and evenings, where their depredations of wheat and gram are considerable. They fly north again in February or March. A vivid impression of their numbers is quoted by Stuart Baker:

> On March 25 C. and I went out after them. They were a sight worth seeing and hearing. There seemed to be vast divisions of them about, but we only 'shikared' one division; while they were feeding there was a broad band of them for about 1½ miles. When alarmed they bunched together and looked just like a white pebble beach about 100 by 500 yards in extent, and when they rose the noise was like the roaring of the sea. We shot three which were all Demoiselles.

Back in Russia, several fascinating features of this bird's habits have been recorded. Again Stuart Baker:

> They arrive in the south of Russia about the beginning of March, in flocks of between two and three hundred individuals. Arriving at the end of their journey, the flock keep together for some time; and even when they have dispersed in couples, they reassemble every morning and evening, preferring in calm weather to exercise themselves by dancing. For this purpose they choose a convenient place, generally the flat shore of a stream. There they stand in a line or in many rows, and begin their games and extraordinary dances, which are not a little surprising to the spectator. They dance and jump around each other, bowing in a burlesque manner, advancing their necks, raising the feathers on the neck-tufts, and half unfolding the wings. In the meantime another set are disputing in a race the prize for swiftness. Arriving at the winning-post they turn back, and walk slowly, and with gravity; all the rest of the company saluting them with reiterated cries, inclinations of the head, and other demonstrations, which are reciprocated. After having

done this for some time, they all rise in the air, where slowly sailing, they describe circles, like the swan and other cranes. After some weeks these assemblies cease, and from that time they are constantly seen walking in pairs together....

Another curiosity is that, possibly to assist camouflage, these birds apparently often construct their nests with small stones, or at least collect a number of small stones in and around the slight hollow or scrape of which their nests are formed. Two eggs are the normal clutch, which appear to require incubation for a month or so, in which both birds participate. Hatching takes place in May or June, and the families remain close-knit until well into July or August, when they begin to gather again into flocks preparatory to the flight south.

# The Eastern Common Crane

## (Grus grus lilfordi)

Finally, there is the Eastern Common Crane, which is a common winter visitor to northern India, often in company with the Demoiselle Crane. Appreciable flocks of both species at one time visited Bharatpur and fed within the Park, but only a few score are now to be seen at any one time, and they tend merely to roost in the Park by night and to feed in surrounding fields by day. This is somewhat of a contrast to the large concentrations which are to be seen in other North Indian inland waters, for example at Sultanpur near Delhi and along the Chambal River not far south of Bharatpur. The Eastern variant of the Common Crane is a slightly lighter grey in colour than the race which is well known to the European observer, but both share the distinctive black head and neck, the broad white band down the cheek and side of the neck, and the red patch of bare skin on the crown. The Common Crane arrives in India in late September or October from its breeding grounds in eastern Siberia and Turkestan, and leaves again in March or early April. It shares with the other crane species the impressive characteristics of the whole family—the vast migratory congregations, the life-long pairing, the elaborate dances and the sonorous, far-carrying trumpeting. A memory which will long remain with me is of a quiet winter morning in the Bharatpur marshes, when I was out walking before dawn. Suddenly the hush was broken by the trumpeting of a large company of cranes out across the marshes. For some minutes nothing was to be seen, but then the trumpeting grew louder as the cranes took flight, until skein after skein rose over the treetops in the dim light of dawn. A procession of skeins passed overhead amid a cacophony of sound, which subsided gradually as they flew on and away towards their daytime feeding grounds.

# PELICANS & FLAMINGOS

THERE ARE generally some pelicans to be seen at Bharatpur in the winter months, although they do not throng there, at least these days, in the numbers in which they are to be found elsewhere in northern India. In 1979, the density of fish in the much reduced lakes and marshes attracted them in large numbers, and flocks of up to 500 were not unusual. In normal years, however, while flocks of up to fifty are not uncommon, numbers fluctuate considerably from day to day. Sometimes only a handful are to be found, often fishing, soaring or roosting in company with Painted Storks. While their mobility is quite poor on land and they generally confine their activity ashore to standing around in groups on sandbanks or bunds, they take off with remarkable ease considering their size, and they fly

Opposite: *Flamingos are among the world's most beautiful and exotic birds. The Greater Flamingo (Phoenicopterus roseus) congregates chiefly in the Rann of Kutch, but outside the breeding season is seen dispersed in flocks across the sub-continent.*

Bottom: *A flock of Rosy Pelicans taking off on an early morning sortie.*

strongly, often making use of thermals to attain considerable heights. They are equally impressive on water, catching fish by swimming strongly and buoyantly, and scooping them up in their pouches. They often fish in a group, driving the fish before them and dipping in unison to make their catch. They are some of the largest birds anywhere, the wingspan of the White Pelican stretching up to three metres from tip to tip. Their cooperative method of fishing reflects their habit of orderly gregariousness. Thus they always face the same direction when standing and fly in precisely spaced formations.

The most common species of pelican at Bharatpur, as elsewhere in northern India, is the White or Rosy Pelican (*Pelecanus onocrotalus*). This is partly a winter migrant, its breeding areas stretching from the Balkans through the Middle East to the lakes of Central Asia. There is, however, also a breeding colony in the Rann of Kutch, at the seaward end of the frontier between India and Pakistan. It is a large white bird with a yellow pouch attached to the underside of a huge bluish bill. The wing pattern is distinctive, with black primaries and, underneath, a black trailing edge to the wings. The name Rosy Pelican derives from the rosy flush which pervades the plumage during the breeding season. The Spot-billed or Grey Pelican (*Pelecanus phillippensis*), which is only a rare visitor to Bharatpur, is, on the other hand, found only in the Indian sub-continent and Burma. This is a slightly smaller bird, grey in colour and lacking the black in the wings. The bill is a fleshy colour with large blue-black spots, and the pouch is a dull purple. There are nesting colonies of this pelican in southern India, as well as in Sri Lanka and Burma, and it is probably something of a local migrant. E.W. Oates, one of the authors of the Bird volumes of the *Fauna of British India*, late in the last century, described a huge breeding colony in the forests of the Sittang in Burma which he estimated to extend over an area no less than thirty kilometres long and eight kilometres wide. The number of birds in the colony, which included Adjutant Storks as well as pelicans, he believed to run into millions. Nests were built high in the forest, between three and twenty in each tree. It is doubtful if any such huge colonies still exist today.

The Dalmatian Pelican (*Pelecanus crispus*) is also a winter visitor to Bharatpur and North India. As the name implies, it is found in south-eastern Europe, but its range extends through Turkey and southern Russia to Central Asia. This bird too is grey in colour, but with a yellowish breast, and the bill is a dark grey over an orange pouch. Some are generally to be found in Bharatpur most winters, but never in large numbers.

# Flamingos

Although the Lesser Flamingo (*Phoeniconaias minor*) has been seen on rare occasions in the Delhi area, the species with which we are concerned at Bharatpur is the Greater Flamingo (*Phoenicopterus ruber roseus*). This long-legged and long-necked bird stands about four feet high, a rosy white in colour with a large down-turned pink bill with a black tip. In flight its white plumage contrasts with brilliant scarlet wings edged with black—a striking and beautiful sight. It breeds in its thousands in 'Flamingo City' in the Rann of Kutch, where its nest consists of conical mounds of mud up to about thirty centimetres in height and hollowed out at the top, stretching at intervals of a few feet over wide expanses of the Rann. Breeding tends to depend on the water conditions in the Rann, but is normally during the autumn or in early spring. Outside these periods the flamingos disperse across the sub-continent in flocks of varying size, and they can be seen at almost any time of the year on suitable marshes or stretches of inland water. Again, water conditions are probably the determining factor governing this movement, and at Bharatpur small flocks of flamingos are most usually to be seen in summer, before the onset of the monsoon, at a time when the water is fairly low and brackish, and seemingly favourable for the gathering of the small crustaceans, larvae, molluscs, seeds and organic particles on which these birds feed.

The flamingo's method of feeding is unique: it inverts its head and immerses it in the water, its angled beak thus being positioned so that it can be used to stir up the mud and filter out food particles through sieve-like plates along the edges of its bill. If not resting, often on a single leg and with head and neck coiled into the back, a party of flamingos is usually to be seen pacing slowly across a stretch of shallow water, some moving their inverted heads from side to side in the ooze and others keeping up a constant gabbling. Their call while on the wing is rather like that of geese, and they fly similarly in a V or echelon formation, with heads and legs stretched out and drooping a little below the body and wings. It is not surprising that they have earned in India the name *Raj Hans*—'King Goose'.

# GEESE

TWO SPECIES of geese visit Bharatpur during the winter, the Eastern race of the Greylag Goose (*Anser anser rubrirostris*) and the Bar-headed Goose (*Anser indicus*). The Greylag is of course well known to Western observers: it is resident in Britain in both wild and feral populations, and also migrates here from Iceland, while on the continent it ranges from Scandinavia and the Baltic through western and eastern Europe to Spain and North Africa. Beyond the Black Sea the Eastern form takes over, but representatives of both sub-species, as well as intermediates, are found in Central Europe through to European Russia, and (as noted earlier) it is not possible to draw a hard and fast line between the two. The Eastern race breeds in considerable numbers in Kazakhstan and around the Aral Sea, and probably also across Siberia and Manchuria. Its wintering areas stretch from the shores of the Caspian Sea through Iraq and Iran to Pakistan, India, Burma and southern China.

The Eastern sub-species is distinctive in being slightly larger and lighter in colour than its Western counterpart, and it has a pink rather than an orange bill. Large flocks winter at Bharatpur, feeding quietly on the marshes or in the surrounding countryside. They tend to lead a lazy life by day, resting or floating around in a leisurely fashion, while in the evenings they fly out to graze in the neighbouring fields, where the winter crops form their favourite diet. But they are always wary, however soporific they may appear, and they raise the noisiest of hullabaloos when disturbed. They seem also to have their moments of *joie de vivre*, since they are very occasionally to be seen indulging in wild aerobatics, diving, rolling and side-slipping, apparently just for the hell of it. Both on migration and in flight to and from their grazing grounds, their honking is unforgettable.

Slightly smaller and even shyer, but altogether more attractive in appearance, is the Bar-headed Goose. This is a pale grey-brown bird with striking black and white markings on the head and neck. Two parallel black bars run at an angle back across the head, one from eye to eye and the other, rather smaller, lower down across the nape, while a white band stretches down the sides of a dark-brown neck. The legs, feet and beak are a contrasting yellow, the beak having a black nail.

Several hundreds of these birds winter at Bharatpur, settling in

Opposite: *The Greylag Goose* (Anser anser) *is a winter visitor to Bharatpur from Europe, where it is the most numerous and widespread of geese and the ancestor of most farmyard geese. Greylag are extremely vigilant, highly gregarious, and given to performing spectacular aerobatic displays.*

*The Bar-headed Goose* (Anser indicus) *is another winter visitor to Bharatpur from its breeding grounds in Tibet. Its powerful wings, longer in proportion to its size than those of any other goose, enable it to fly at incredible heights in its southward migration across the Himalayas.*

flocks varying in size from a dozen or so to over a hundred. They are very difficult to approach, resting in safe areas during the day and feeding in nearby fields during the evening and night, where they are reputed to cause even more damage to crops than the Greylag. Their winter range seems to be confined chiefly to northern India and Pakistan across to Bangladesh and Assam, while their breeding grounds are to be found on the high lakes of Central Asia. Ringing records are few, but connect lakes in Kirghizia in the USSR, near the border with China, with wintering areas in Gilgit and Pakistan. Other breeding sites have been reported on swamps and lakes in Ladakh, Tibet, western China and Mongolia. An appreciable decline in numbers has been noted over recent years and there seems little doubt that this has occurred in Tibet in particular. There, the geese had been reputed to have become extremely tame, as would be expected in a country where all forms of life were regarded as sacred, and so the effect on them of the Chinese invasion is likely to have been severe.

Both these species of geese arrive in India in October or November, the Greylag being on the whole a little earlier than the Bar-headed, and both are gone by the end of March. Both migrate over the Himalayas, where Dr Salim Ali reports them as having been seen at Dehra Doon, in the foothills, at a height of 9,000 metres, this observation having been made by telescope during the spring

migration as they crossed the face of the moon. There was also an extremely interesting account some years ago by C. H. Donald of migrating Bar-headed Geese which he observed while on hunting trips high in Kashmir. These he consistently sighted in considerable numbers shortly after sundown, but rather later in the evening during the autumn migration than on the return in the spring. Judging the direction of their flight over the plateau on which he was hunting, he reckoned that their breeding grounds were probably the great Tibetan lakes of Pangong and Tso Morari to the north-east, and that they were dropping down to, or coming from, the Chenab river, where it flows out of the hills into the North Indian plain. Reviewing the alternative passes and river valleys available in the area, he concluded that the geese were taking the most direct route rather than several which would have been easier, even though it involved the crossing of several mountain ranges at heights of between 4,500—5,000 metres. The later timing of the autumn passage he accounted for by reckoning that his vantage point was nearer their point of entry to the Indian plains than to the breeding areas, presumably on the assumption that the geese started their migration late in the day and flew largely by night. This view, that geese and, indeed, other migrating birds, are content to take as their route the shortest distance between two points, even if it means crossing high mountain ranges, seems now to be generally accepted.

*Geese are among the most powerful fliers in the avian world, and extremely wary of predators—hence the proverbial difficulty of 'wild-goose-chasing'*

# DUCKS

AS WE HAVE seen, Bharatpur was created expressly to provide a permanent habitat for ducks; and these are still one of its major attractions, although, sadly, numbers have diminished in recent years. Nevertheless, considerable flocks still arrive each winter and several resident species are to be found on the marshes all the year round. A fair amount of ringing has been undertaken at Bharatpur over recent years, and this has provided substantial evidence of the migration of the visiting species. The greater number come across the Himalayas and the Hindu Kush from Kazakhstan and areas of the Soviet Union south and east of the Caspian and Aral Seas, but a proportion also travel from much further afield in Central Asia and Siberia. With few exceptions, they are all species which will be familiar to European observers; they include the Ruddy Shelduck ( *Tadorna ferruginea*), Common Shelduck ( *Tadorna tadorna*), Marbled Teal ( *Marmaronetta angustirostris*), Common Teal ( *Anas crecca crecca*), Mallard ( *Anas platyrhynchos*), Gadwall ( *Anas strepera strepera*), Falcated Teal ( *Anas falcata*), Wigeon ( *Anas penelope*), Garganey ( *Anas querquedela*), Shoveler ( *Anas clypeata*), Red-crested Pochard ( *Netta rufina*), Common Pochard ( *Aythya ferina*), White-eyed Pochard ( *Aythya nyroca*) and Tufted Duck ( *Aythya fuligula*).

Of these waterfowl, the Ruddy Shelduck, a largish, attractive orange-brown duck with a buff head and neck, is a visitor to Bharatpur in modest numbers, and flocks of up to thirty or so are generally to be seen in the winter months. The Common Shelduck, on the other hand, is an uncommon visitor and is to be seen only rarely. Hugh Whistler recounts the rather charming Indian legend about the Ruddy Shelduck, which derives from the fact that although this bird is generally to be seen in pairs, the pair tend to separate from time to time, especially when feeding at night. The legend suggests that they are the reincarnation of erring lovers who are condemned to remain in sight of each other but always separated by intervening water. The call of the Ruddy Shelduck, which is a raucously noisy bird and given to duetting, is reduced for the purpose of the legend to form the names Chakwa and Chakwi, and the lovers are said eternally to ask the question, '*Chakwa, aun?*' (Chakwa, shall I come?) and to give the answer, '*Chakwi na ao!*'

Opposite: *A flight of Shoveler Ducks* (Anas clypeata). *This duck derives its name from its distinctive broad, shovel-shaped beak. It arrives in Bharatpur around October from its breeding grounds in Europe and is among the last of the migrants to leave. The Shoveler's rank flesh makes it unappealing as a table bird.*

Top: *The Ruddy Shelduck* (Tadorna ferruginea) *or Brahminy Duck, as it is known in India, is one of the world's most widespread birds, being found from Morocco to China. It arrives in Bharatpur in winter from its high-altitude home in Ladakh and Tibet.*

Bottom: *The Pintail* (Anas acuta) *is a winter visitor which arrives around October from the Caspian region and Siberia. Its sporting qualities and delicious meat make it a favourite target of hunters.*

(Chakwi, do not come!). The Ruddy Shelduck breeds as far south as Tibet and Ladakh, as well as further to the north in Central Asia and to the east in Mongolia and China.

Of the other migrant ducks, the Pintail winters at Bharatpur in large numbers, often resting on the marshes in close company with the Greylag Geese. The Wigeon, Shoveler and Common Teal are also numerous, but the Garganey tends to be a bird of passage, passing through Bharatpur from August to October and again in March-April, but spending its winters further south. Both the Tufted Duck and the White-eyed Pochard are also common visitors, as are the Red-crested and Common Pochards. The Mallard, on the other hand, strikes the visitor from Europe as relatively scarce, perhaps because it tends to winter in Kashmir, where it also breeds in small numbers. The Marbled Teal and Falcated Teal are also quite rare.

Of the resident ducks, the one which is exclusive to the Indian sub-continent is the Indian race of the Spot-billed Duck (*Anas poecilorhyncha poecilorhyncha*), so called because it has a prominent red spot on each side of the base of the bill and a yellow tip. It is a large duck, rather resembling an ungainly version of the Mallard. Overall it is a fawn grey in colour merging to blackish-brown on the wings, back and tail. The crown and a broad eye-stripe are blackish, the bill is black with a yellow tip, and the bird also shows a conspicuous white and metallic green speculum, with a broad white

*The Spotbill Duck* (Anas poecilorhyncha) *is a resident duck, also prized by sportsmen though deplored by farmers. It dives only to evade capture, preferring to get its food (chiefly vegetable matter) from paddies or marshland.*

bar above. It is a rather silent and somewhat stand-offish bird, rarely found in company with other species, and normally associating with its own species only in pairs or small parties.

A rather larger resident duck is the Nukta, or Comb-Duck (*Sarkidiornis melanotus melanotus*). This bird can readily be seen at Bharatpur, partly because it is not infrequently to be found roosting in trees in fairly substantial numbers, and partly because it moves around more freely by day than do most geese and ducks. It is a handsome bird, the head and neck white spotted with black, the wings and tail black glossed with purple, green and blue, the breast white and the flanks a pale, ashy grey. The male has an obtrusive knob or comb on its bill, variable in size but largest when breeding. It is a strong flier and is also a relatively noisy bird, particularly in the breeding season. It is found in sub-Saharan Africa and Malagasy as well as in the Indian sub-continent and Burma.

At the other end of the scale in terms of size is the Cotton Teal or Indian Pygmy Goose (*Nettapus coromandelianus*), which is to be found not only in India but also in China and South-east Asia through to New Guinea. Far from being a pygmy goose, it is in fact a pygmy duck, at some thirty-three centimetres in length the smallest duck anywhere. The male is a very attractive bird, particularly in the breeding season, when the blackish upper plumage is glossed with green and purple, and the head, neck and underparts are white. The crown and forehead are also black, while a low black collar and white wing bar are other distinguishing marks. In the female, and the male in his non-breeding plumage, the back is brownish and the remainder of the body mottled brown. This too is a perching duck and makes its nest in a tree, but it is most often to be seen on the water in flocks or small groups, preferring areas with good cover and plenty of vegetation. It flies low and fast, and can jink and turn with ease and rapidity.

Lastly there is the Lesser Whistling Teal (*Dendrocygna javanica*), a small, rather inconspicuous duck, chestnut and brown on the upper parts, and chestnut paling to light brown on the flanks and underparts. Its name derives from the sibilant, double-noted call which it utters constantly when on the wing. It is a good swimmer and is fairly mobile on land, but its preference is to roost on trees, in which it also nests. It is not seen at Bharatpur in the large flocks in which it occurs elsewhere in India, but small parties are present from time to time.

# OTHER
# WATERBIRDS

A VARIETY of other waterbirds throng the marshes at Bharatpur, most of them residents but with some migrants among their number. Among the most prominent are the jacanas, of which two species are to be found, the Bronze-winged Jacana (*Metopidius indicus*) and the Pheasant-tailed Jacana (*Hydrophasianus chirugus*). The former is glossy black over the head, back and abdomen, and olive-bronze over the back and wings. It has a short chestnut tail and a distinctive white stripe over and behind each eye. Its elongated toes and claws enable it, like other jacanas, to support itself on surface plants, and it is almost always to be found on ponds and marshes which are thick with vegetation. It can swim and dive when necessary, but it almost always prefers to pad around in its search for food. When alarmed, its reaction is to freeze, either stretching itself out among the vegetation or half-submerging itself for better concealment. It is resident in the Indian sub-continent and through South-east Asia to Indonesia.

The Pheasant-tailed Jacana has a wider range. It is found on lakes in Kashmir and among the Himalayas on the one hand, and as far east as China and the Philippines on the other. In its breeding plumage it is an attractive bird, with a long down-curved tail and a prominent yellow patch on the hind neck. The head, front of the neck and wings are white and the remainder of the body dark brown. In winter it is relatively drab, its plumage being mostly brown and white, and the 'pheasant' tail is missing. Particularly at that season it resembles the Paddy Bird in being well concealed by its drab colouring until it is compelled to fly, when it is transformed by a sudden flash of white wings. It is less shy than the Bronze-winged Jacana and is more often to be seen paddling around in open water. Both species are polyandrous, the males establishing territories, building the nests and incubating the eggs, which the female Jacana will lay in clutches for a succession of husbands, possibly, in the case of the Pheasant-tailed species, for as many as ten in all during the season.

Coots and moorhens also abound at Bharatpur. The coots (*Fulica atra*) are especially numerous in winter, when the residents are

*The Bronze-winged Jacana* (Metopidius indicus) *is another resident found in most parts of India where floating aquatic vegetation abounds. Its stilt-like legs and long toes are adaptations to its mode of foraging for food—tripping across lily-pads—hence also its alternative name of 'lily-trotter'.*

joined by large numbers of migrants from Central and western Asia. A recent ringing recovery suggests that some also come from China, while others migrate from as far away as the upper reaches of the Ob river in the Tomsk region. The Common Moorhens (*Gallinula chloropus indica*) also very much resemble the European variety, although they tend to be a little smaller. A larger and more spectacular bird is the Purple Moorhen (*Porphyrio porphyrio poliocephalus*), a blue and purple bird with a red forehead and bill and a white patch under its tail. It is found not only throughout the Indian sub-continent, but also as far east as Indo-China. At Bharatpur it can sometimes be seen in sizeable parties, but more commonly singly or in pairs. It is a weak flier and much prefers to scrabble among the reedbeds, which it does in a typically moorhen manner, bobbing its head and flicking its tail as it pokes around. It is sometimes to be seen perched rather precariously on reeds, preening or sunning itself. It is a noisy bird, particularly during the mating

season, when the male courts the female by flourishing a beak-full of reeds, bowing to her and chuckling loudly.

Perhaps more common throughout India than any other species of waterfowl is the White-breasted Waterhen (*Amaurornis phoenicurus*). This is a bird of about the same size as a moorhen, with long legs and toes. It has a conspicuous white face and breast, slaty-olive upper plumage and chestnut underparts. It too flashes its chestnut tail in moorhen fashion as it stalks around the undergrowth. It tends to be a pugnacious bird and can be extremely noisy in the breeding season. One observer has described its call as follows: 'It began with loud, harsh roars which might have been elicited from a bear by roasting it slowly over a large fire, then suddenly changed to a clear note repeated like the cooing of a dove.' Slightly overstated, perhaps, but it does at times emit a somewhat harsh call, while at others it produces a repeated sharp metallic note which it is capable of keeping up all night long.

*The Purple Moorhen (Porphyrio porphyrio) is a resident gallinule that skulks in dense reed-beds and wades over matted floating vegetation in search of food. The male's courtship display consists of 'gifts' of waterweeds, accompanied with elaborate bows and noisy chuckles.*

# EAGLES
# & HARRIERS

FOUR SPECIES of eagle, the Pallas's Fishing Eagle, the Short-toed Eagle, the Lesser Spotted Eagle and Tawny Eagle, are resident at Bharatpur, while one other, the Crested Serpent Eagle, is a local migrant. Several other species which breed in Central Asia move down from the mountains at the onset of winter, to coincide with the arrival of the migrants on which they mostly prey. The winter visitors include the Greater Spotted Eagle, Imperial Eagle, Bonelli's Hawk Eagle and Steppe Eagle. The White-tailed Sea Eagle also occasionally visits Bharatpur. Particularly in the winter months, eagles are a constant delight to the observer as he makes his way around the Park. Sometimes soaring high above, sometimes swooping low over the marshes in search of prey, but more often just perched in a large tree surveying the scene or keeping guard over a nest, they are not the least of the glories of Bharatpur. To select from my notes only one of many thrilling sights, happening to look up on a sunny winter's morning when the thermals were developing strongly, I saw circling above two Greater Spotted Eagles, an Imperial Eagle, two Short-toed Eagles and, for good measure, a Brahminy Kite. If I single out four species of eagle for special mention, it is on somewhat arbitrary grounds.

## Pallas's or Ring-tailed Fishing Eagle
### (Haliaeetus leucoryphus)

This magnificent eagle, which is of the same genus as the American Bald Eagle and, like it, has a markedly flattened crown, is a familiar sight at Bharatpur, where two pairs nest in winter in isolated trees standing in the marshes. It is easily recognised by.its pale golden head and neck, which contrast with the dark brown of the remainder of its plumage, and by the broad white band across its tail towards the tip. The male, which is slightly smaller than the female, takes turns in incubating the eggs and feeding the young, and hunting too is often a joint venture. The range of these eagles is not accurately

Opposite: *The Crested Serpent Eagle* (Spilornis cheela) *is a large, dark brown eagle with a black and white nuchal crest which flares into a handsome ruff when the bird is alarmed. Its three- or four-note screaming whistle can be distinguished even when it is a speck in the sky.*

Overleaf: *The Black-winged Kite* (Elanus ceruleus) *is a magnificent grey, white and black bird, widely resident in the sub-continent but patchily distributed. It can often be seen perched on telegraph poles or hovering for prey.*

known, but considerable numbers appear to spend their summers in the Tibetan uplands and have been seen notably in the Kailas-Lake Manasarovar area, a place of Hindu pilgrimage which has recently been reopened by the Chinese authorities. The suggestion is that, unusually, these eagles migrate south in the winter in order to breed, exchanging their frozen upland lakes for a habitat in which there are ample fish for eating and trees for nesting. Their nests at Bharatpur are, typically, large, untidy platforms of branches and twigs, which are rebuilt and reused year after year, each pair jealously guarding their hunting territory. One pair has repeatedly bred successfully in recent years, but the other has failed to do so, notwithstanding that the female has appeared with a new male two years in succession. It remains to be seen if the latest male will succeed where his two predecessors failed.

The cry of this eagle is as distinctive as its appearance—a raucous

*The Greater Spotted Eagle* (Aquila clanga) *is a resident raptor affecting well-watered and wooded areas. It is usually seen perched singly on a tree-top on the look-out for prey. It actively hunts waterfowl (coots and moorhens being preferred) by menacing and scattering a flock, then isolating an individual victim and stooping on it repeatedly.*

shriek which has been likened to the creak of an ungreased cartwheel or the unoiled wooden block of a village well, both sounds familiar in the Indian countryside. It has also been likened to a hoarse Pekinese barking, a description which will doubtless provide a sure means of identification for owners of Pekinese dogs susceptible to colds. My own impression is that the cry is somewhat like that of a Herring Gull, but with a little extra 'edge' to it. As with so many eagles, a pair in the breeding season will put on a particularly noisy performance as they wheel and tumble overhead.

When hunting fish, this eagle will search most often in shallow water, since, unlike for example the Osprey, it does not plunge but takes its prey in its talons from near the surface. There is on record an instance of a Pallas's Fishing Eagle seizing a fish weighing no less that six kilograms, its technique with a fish too large to carry being to drag it along the surface until it can beach it on the margin of the lake. It also preys on waterfowl and, like the Marsh Harrier, often first attracts the attention of the observer by its progressive disturbance and scattering of birds across the surface of a marsh as it glides low overhead. Sometimes a pair will isolate a coot or moorhen and stoop on it continually until it is finally too exhausted to dive and can be taken on the surface. On other occasions it robs other birds, such as cormorants and harriers. In Bharatpur particularly, it preys on injured geese and ducks, as well as on the young of the nesting birds such as the ibises and storks, and it has even been known to take Demoiselle Cranes. All in all, this eagle provides one of the finest spectacles of Bharatpur, where fortunately the variety and abundance of the available food ensures that it lives a tolerably secure existence.

# Greater & Lesser Spotted Eagles
## (Aquila clanga & Aquila pomarina)

Although of the two species of Spotted Eagles, the Greater Spotted is said to be the one which is particularly drawn to marshland, while the Lesser Spotted prefers dry, open country, both are to be found at Bharatpur, more often than not surveying the scene from perches on the edges of the marshes. It is not easy to distinguish the two, or to distinguish either of them from Tawny and Steppe Eagles, particularly if they should be adult birds at rest, when they appear an all too uniform brown all over. As between the two adult Spotted Eagles, the Greater Spotted has underwing coverts which are normally darker than the flight feathers, while the reverse is the case with the Lesser Spotted. The Greater Spotted also has seven 'fingers' at the extremities of the wings, while the Lesser Spotted has only six, although I defy anyone to be sure of counting the difference beyond a shadow of doubt under normal observation conditions! Immature

Top: *The Brahminy Kite*
(Haliastur indus) *is a
common resident which
prefers the neighbourhood of
water but occasionally adopts
a scavenging existence
around human habitations. It
seizes dead or surface-
floating fish, sometimes
consuming them in flight,
and—being a diffident
bird—is subject to piracy by
crows and other kites.*

Bottom: *The Marsh Harrier*
(Circus aeruginosus) *is a
winter visitor from Europe
and Mongolia, a graceful flier
with a distinctive leisurely
flight sweeping low over the
water.*

birds are a little less difficult, since the Greater Spotted tends to have extensive spotting on the back, while the Lesser Spotted has very much less. However, odd variants of all four species exist and, while the exception may prove the rule, it is all too likely to undermine the confidence of the observer.

The summer breeding grounds of the Greater Spotted Eagle stretch from eastern Europe through European Russia to Siberia, while it winters from Spain and the Mediterranean area through Iran to India and China. In India, it has been particularly susceptible to the draining of marshland, and its winter refuge at Bharatpur is assuming greater importance as the years pass. The Lesser Spotted is found somewhat further to the west in Europe, whence it winters in tropical Africa, but its range in Central and South Asia is very similar to that of the Greater Spotted species. Both species are notable for their wild 'kyak-kyak' cry, the Lesser Spotted's version being more high-pitched than that of the Greater Spotted: it has been well described as resembling the barking of a small dog.

# Crested Serpent Eagle

(Spilornis cheela)

This eagle is resident in the Indian sub-continent, although it may indulge in some local migration or at least wandering. It is an immensely attractive bird, distinguished, when alarmed, by its prominent fan-shaped crest, composed of black feathers with white bars along their edges. Hardly less conspicuous is a bright yellow patch at the base of the bill, matched by deep yellow eyes set in a dark face and heavily scaled yellow legs. The upper parts are dark brown, relieved by lighter spots or edgings to the feathers, while the underparts are a lighter cinnamon brown, barred or ocellated in white. In flight it can be identified by its broad, rounded wings, which are held well back, as well as by a very broad white stripe along the wings and a white bar across the tail. It likes to perch bolt upright in a tree, where it remains partly concealed in the foliage while enjoying a clear view of the surrounding countryside. It is also often seen soaring, sometimes at immense heights, and a pair in the breeding season can be seen tumbling and circling in aerobatic display. Even more arresting is its high-pitched whistling scream, uttered both while soaring and from its perch. Its diet of small mammals appears frequently to include snakes and it has been seen killing cobras. In the nesting season, when a pair raise a single chick, the adult digests its prey only partially and then regurgitates it for its young.

# Harriers

Two other winter visitors to Bharatpur, both from Central Asia, are the Marsh Harrier (*Circus aeruginosus*) and the Pale Harrier (*Circus macrourus*). Of the two, the Marsh Harrier is the more conspicuous and is often to be seen as it sits alone on a bank or among the reeds, or as it silently quarters the marshes at a height of some six or nine metres, scattering flocks of wildfowl as it passes overhead. The male is a most attractive bird, with silvery grey wings and tail, a mixture of buff, rufous and brown on the head, body and upper wing coverts, and the outer flight feathers black. Female and juvenile birds are an overall dark brown with creamy buff markings on the head and leading edge of the wings. The Marsh Harrier's flight is most distinctive, consisting of a few regular flaps of the wings followed by a slow glide, in the course of which it banks and turns as it searches for its prey. It feeds on frogs, fish and small mammals, but has been known to take sizeable birds such as Coots, moorhens and Pond Herons. It is one of the sportsman's major bugbears, often putting up birds well out of gunshot or taking wounded birds in front of the guns. At times it enjoys soaring on V-shaped wings. It arrives in India in September and is gone again in late March or early April.

The Pale Harrier is a rather more elegant bird, with pale grey upper parts and even paler, almost whitish, head and underparts. Its wings are narrower and more pointed than those of the Marsh Harrier and have black tips. The female is a rich brown above with streaked brown upper tail coverts: the underparts are a lighter brown and there is a light buff collar behind dark ear coverts. I have not myself seen this harrier within the Park, but have sighted it more than once in its more usual habitat just outside, hunting over open farmland. It does so by gliding only a few feet above the ground, conforming to the contours of the land and banking around obstacles. Like a low-level bomber, its tactics are clearly to hit the target with a minimum of forewarning. When it sights its prey it turns and pounces quickly and silently. Although it hunts singly, it roosts on open ground, often with other harrier species and sometimes in surprising numbers, each bird spacing itself a few feet apart from its neighbour. The migration habits of this bird are intriguing: the Pale Harriers which winter in India come from Central Asia, but others from much the same breeding area travel as far afield as West and South Africa, their journeys extending to as much as 8,000 kilometres. A main migration route runs down the Nile Valley and thence down the Rift Valley in East Africa. Observations in northern India suggest that the migrating birds do not fly in flocks, but that they make their way individually along the migration route, congregating each evening and resuming their separate journeys the following day.

Overleaf: *The Eastern Steppe Eagle* (Aquila rapax), *also a winter visitor from Central Asia, has a relatively slow and heavy flight but is adept at snatching prey from other eagles and hawks.*

Pg. 85, top: *Bharatpur falls in the winter range of the Long-legged Buzzard* (Buteo rufinus) *which breeds in the Himalayas. This bird frequently congregates at the site of jungle fires in pursuit of fleeing insects, lizards etc. and is noted for its spectacular aerial displays.*

Pg. 85, bottom: *The Indian Sparrow-hawk* (Accipiter risus) *descends to the plains in winter from its north-western Himalayan habitat. A solitary raptor, it preys chiefly on other birds (in this case a dove), pouncing on its quarry from a tree-top and devouring it on the ground.*

# VULTURES

N O BOOK about Indian birds would be adequate without at least
a mention of vultures, if only because the Indian landscape never
seems complete without the sight of one or more wheeling
magnificently in the blue, alert for signs of death in the towns,
villages and countryside below. Revulsion at their manners and
appearance is understandable but of course misplaced: they are in
fact merely—but splendidly—adapted in form and habit to that
particular niche in the natural order in which they can survive, while
they provide an invaluable social service in removing carcasses and
offal which would otherwise putrify in the tropical heat. The attitude
of mind which compares a vulture unfavourably with, say, an eagle
would seem to reflect the more general prejudice against scavengers,

Opposite: *The large, broad
wings of most species of
vulture give them the ability
to soar effortlessly for hours
high in the sky. Vultures are
prolific in the tropical
countries of Asia and Africa,
where carrion is abundant.
A White-backed Vulture
taking off from the nest,
showing its distinctive white
bands under the wings.*

Bottom: *The King Vulture,
distinguished by its naked
red head and turkey-like
wattles.*

Opposite: *A rear view of the King Vulture (Torgus calvus)—a powerfully built bird, as its name implies.*

Top: *The Egyptian Vulture (Neophron percnopterus), a resident and partially migratory bird, is also known as the 'Pharaoh's Chicken'. It is a highly effective scavenger of carrion, offal, garbage and even human excrement.*

Bottom: *The White-backed Vulture (Gyps bengalensis) is the commonest resident vulture. Its feeding habits are revolting to humans, but it makes an effort to keep itself clean, being fond of bathing and drying out its wings cormorant-fashion.*

bird or mammal, and the equally irrational predeliction for species which kill.

Another common but dubious conception about vultures is that the skill and rapidity with which they can detect death, whether actual or approaching, is somehow uncanny. Certainly they must have remarkable eyesight, but a description of the events which normally surround death in the tropics goes far towards deflating the mystique and providing a more mundane explanation of the phenomenon. Thus when an animal dies, or even while it is dying, it is soon found by the ubiquitous crows or pariah dogs, if not by both, and the presence of a single crow or dog at a carcass soon attracts many more. Because the carcass is likely still to be fresh and unbroken, inevitably there ensues a fair amount of competition and jockeying for position and, at the same time, little opportunity as yet for any quiet, solid feeding. The resulting confusion in turn attracts the equally ubiquitous kites, which wheel and dip above the dead animal, anticipating the opportunity to swoop down and snatch portions of the feast. Activity thus quickly builds up, until it would be surprising if it did not catch the eye of a vulture gliding high in the thermals overhead and prompt it to descend to investigate further. And since vultures keep a watchful eye on one another's movements, the sight of one careering down will quickly attract a widening circle of others.

Perhaps more remarkable is the speed with which vultures can devour a corpse. Thus the account has been recorded of sixty or seventy vultures having stripped the remains of two sloth bears, each weighing not less than 125 kilograms, so thoroughly in the space of a mere forty minutes that late-comers had to stand around disappointed. On another occasion a flock of vultures is recorded as having devoured a whole bullock in twenty minutes flat.

An unnerving experience at Bharatpur is the sudden feeling that one is being watched, the explanation being found when one sees a vulture observing one with a beady eye from the top of a nearby tree, no doubt sizing up one's weight and value as a carcass. Occasionally, this watcher will be the Black or King Vulture (*Torgos calvus*), a magnificent glossy black and brown bird with a naked deep-red head and neck. Other distinguishing marks are white patches on the flanks and at the base of the neck, red patches on the thighs and red wattles hanging down behind the ears. This is a solitary vulture, normally found only in ones or twos, although distributed fairly widely throughout the Indian sub-continent, Burma and South-east Asia.

More commonly, however, the tree-top observer will be the White-backed or Bengal Vulture (*Gyps bengalensis*), a highly gregarious bird and commonest of all the Indian vultures. This is a blackish-brown bird with a bare, slaty-grey head and neck, a white ruff and a white patch on the lower back which provides a sure identification both at rest and in flight. A flock of vultures soaring and circling overhead; a large nesting colony on the outskirts of a town or village; a number roosting together in an avenue of trees along a canal or main road; a crowd jostling around a carcass or standing around so gorged that they can barely fly—these are all common sights in India and all more likely than not to be composed overwhelmingly of the White-backed species.

The other common vulture, the Neophron or Egyptian Vulture (*Neophron percnopterus*), has a much wider range, extending from eastern Europe and North Africa through the Middle East to the Indian sub-continent. It has a naked head and upper neck, the skin of which is a deep yellow, while, with the exception of black flight feathers, the plumage is an overall dirty white. This is an extremely scruffy bird, largely parasitic on man and with a hen-like appearance and habits which have earned it the name of Pharaoh's Chicken'. It is usually to be seen stalking around in ones or twos in the vicinity of human habitation, scavenging just about everything in sight, however unspeakable. If it is notable for anything, it is for being one of the few birds which is a tool-user, in that it has been seen to break open ostrich eggs by throwing stones against them with its bill.

Vultures have been described by one observer as practical but not very pleasant birds. However that may be, they are a part of the Bharatpur scene which it is impossible to overlook.

# OWLS

A pair of Collared Scops Owls (Otus bakkamoena) *which are found in several sub-species all over the sub-continent. The large eyes and cryptic camouflage are characteristic of noctural raptors.*

TOWARDS the eastern boundary of the Bharatpur Park, near Jatoli village, there is a fine grove of Kadam trees, planted there by a former Maharaja. These border the track which leads from Sita Ram Bani temple to the Jatoli canal and provide the most extensive area of mature woodland which the Park possesses. Further south, at the end of the track which leads down to Hans Sarovar, is 'Kadam Kunj', another, smaller grove of Kadam trees standing close to a ruined hunting lodge. Both these stands of woodland provide haunts for some of Bharatpur's less obtrusive species of birds, the owls. Eight species of owls have been seen in the Park, representative of five of the twenty-four owl genera (*Bubo, Otus, Athene, Strix* and *Asio*). None of them, except perhaps the Dusky Horned Owl and the Spotted Owlet, are at all common, and with the thinning of Bharatpur's woodlands, their habitats are slowly being eroded.

The most magnificent of these owls is the Indian Eagle Owl or Great Horned Owl (*Bubo bubo bengalensis*), but by far the most beautiful is the Mottled Wood Owl (*Strix ocellata*), whose markings are so delicate that it is almost impossible to do them justice in words. A particularly fine specimen is on display in the Natural History Museum at South Kensington and is well worth seeing. It is a largish owl, of the same genus as the Tawny Owl and similar to it in shape, although rather bigger. Its facial disc is patterned in concentric circles of white and chocolate brown, with a sprinkling of fluffier, tawny feathers on either side of the eyes. Its head and back are also very delicately mottled in white and dark brown, giving an overall greyish impression, but again there is a sprinkling of lighter brown, particularly over the nape and neck. Under the face is a prominent fluffy half-collar, a soft white in colour, while the underparts are whitish, narrowly barred in dark brown. As camouflage, these markings are incomparably effective, and it is singularly difficult to spot this bird as it perches hidden in the thick woodland canopy.

One of these owls was nesting in the Kadam grove by Jatoli village in the early weeks of 1982, its nest lodged in the fork of a large tree less than six metres above the ground. The hollow of the tree itself appeared to comprise almost all that there was of the nest, which possessed only the minimum of lining. While incubating, the parent bird faced out of the tree on one side, its tail feathers protruding from the other, but a 180° turn of its head enabled it to see out in both directions.

The Mottled Wood Owl is found only in the Indian sub-continent. Although its range there is extensive and it is not uncommon, it seems on the whole to prefer lightly wooded land near cultivation. It is more often identified by its calls, which are a mellow hoot in the non-breeding season and a louder, rather eerie, quavering call while breeding, alternating with the occasional shriek.

The smaller Kadam grove was, during the same winter, the nesting site of two pairs of a rather more spectacular, although less attractive, species of owl, the Dusky Horned Owl (*Bubo coromandus coromandus*). As the Latin name suggests, this is also exclusively a resident of the Indian sub-continent, where it is again well distributed. In Hindi it is called, rather delightfully, *Jungli ghughu*. It is one of the largest owls, a dull greyish-brown colour overall, very finely mottled and spotted with white, and its slim, upright silhouette with vertical, close-set horns is unmistakable. Its call is also distinctive, a series of notes diminishing in loudness and quickening in pace, likened by Dr Salim Ali to a ping-pong ball bouncing to silence.

The two pairs of Dusky Horned Owls nesting at Kadam Kunj showed an interesting diversity in their choice of nests. One pair had taken over a large, untidy structure, probably built orginally by a vulture, standing high in a leafy Kadam tree on the edge of the grove. The other pair, by contrast, had chosen a minimal nest in the low fork of a dead tree standing quite isolated in the nearby marsh. Two chicks were visible in the latter nest, a light fawn in colour—a not unusual number, although normally only the larger chick reaches maturity. A year later, a vulture was back in occupation of the one nest, while the isolated tree holding the other had collapsed into the marsh. Undeterred, one of the pairs of owls had taken over another vulture's nest close to the hunting lodge.

Another spot where owls are generally to be seen is in the centre of the Park, near the Keoladeo Temple. This is normally the haunt of a family of Spotted Owlets (*Athene brama indica*), several of which are often to be seen huddled together on the branch of an overhanging tree. This quaint little owl, brownish in colour and spotted in white, is conspicuous for its relatively large head and bright yellow eyes. It has the odd habit of bobbing up and down as it surveys its surroundings from its perch, possibly in order to obtain a good perspective on any object of interest; and the sight of a row of spotted owlets, all bobbing and peering in random order, is highly comical.

The flight of this owlet is quite distinctive, consisting of a few rapid flaps followed by a dipping glide with its wings pressed close to its sides, as it makes its way from perch to perch. Also rather comical is its habit of chattering and squealing as it emerges from its hole before dusk; but when on the wing it can, like other owls, be ominously silent.

Also near the Keoladeo Temple is the haunt of a pair of Collared Scops Owls (*Otus bakkamoena gangeticus*). This is a delightful little owl with conspicuous ear-tufts, buff-coloured and finely mottled and stippled in dark brown. Its name derives from the markedly paler collar around the back of its neck. It is very nocturnal in its habits and is far more frequently detected by its call, a soft interrogative 'wheet' uttered every few seconds. By day, the pair at the Keoladeo Temple stay concealed high in the branches of a palm tree or deep

in the foliage of nearby acacia.

In Western countries, our feelings about owls tend to be inconsistent. On the one hand, they often excite affection and are regarded as the embodiments of wisdom, an attitude which seems to go back several millenia to ancient Athens. At the same time they have been regarded as ill-omened, an attitude perhaps arising from their nocturnal habits, their alternation of uncanny silence with eerie or even hideous calls, and their propensity to frequent numinous places, such as churchyards. Shakespeare of course reflects this ambivalence:

> Then nightly sings the staring owl,
> Tu-whit, Tu-whoo, a merry note,
> While greasy Joan doth keel the pot.

but:

> It was the owl that shriek'd, the fatal bellman
> That gives the stern'st good night.

Indians have no such ambivalence: for them an owl is a bird of ill-omen and a harbinger of death, and a great number of superstitions exist about it. Many bear on its reputed ability to foretell the future, particularly if this should be pregnant with misfortune.

Opposite: *The magnificent Indian Great Horned Owl* (Bubo bubo) *is a largely nocturnal bird, resident throughout the sub-continent in wooded countryside. Its preference for rodents makes it tremendously beneficial to farmers.*

Top: *The most widely
distributed species of
kingfisher in the
sub-continent is the
handsome White-breasted
Kingfisher* (Halcyon
smryrnensis)*, a frequenter
of both dry and wetland
habitats.*

Bottom: *The Common or
Small Blue Kingfisher* (Alcedo
atthis) *is a common resident
found near streams, canals
and watered tracts, usually
singly or in pairs.*

# KINGFISHERS

THE EXTENSIVE 'bunds' at Bharatpur, with their mix of large and small trees and bushes overhanging clear water and marsh, form an ideal habitat for kingfishers, which occupy numerous territories up and down their banks. Kingfishers, which pair for life, are strongly territorial, and one occasionally comes across a couple glaring pugnaciously at each other from neighbouring perches at the margins of their territories, until one swoops on the other and drives him off. Perhaps the most common, and certainly the most noticeable, species at Bharatpur is the White-breasted Kingfisher (*Halcyon smyrnensis*), the reason for its comparatively high degree of visibility being not just its spectacular colouring but also its habit of perching on reeds out in the marsh as well as in the cover of trees

*The Lesser Pied Kingfisher* (Ceryle rudis), *also a common resident, is easily distinguished by its bold black and white spots and bars. It hauls its catch out to a convenient perch and batters it to death before consuming it.*

and bushes. It is a largish bird, not far short of the size of a pigeon, and is armed with a red bill of formidable length and thickness. Its head, neck and lower plumage are reddish brown in colour, its throat and breast white, and its upper plumage a brilliant cobalt blue. A white patch is prominent on the wing when it flies. It is a noisy bird, with a call which has variously been described as a 'rattling scream' and a 'loud screaming laugh'. It feeds not just on fish, but also on prey such as lizards and grasshoppers, and even on small birds such as sparrows and munias, and it is in fact not uncommonly seen away from water among farmland and woods.

A kingfisher of similar size, but with contrasting colouring and somewhat differing habits is the Pied Kingfisher (*Ceryle rudis*). This is a smart black and white bird, spotted and streaked over the head, back and tail, but with a predominance of white on the underparts. The male has two black stripes across the breast, but the female only one, broken in the middle. Unlike the White-breasted Kingfisher, its diet is wholly aquatic, and while it also perches while looking for its prey, it is distinctive for its more frequent practice of hovering above the water as it hunts. It can remain stationary for appreciable periods, with rapidly vibrating wings and with beak and tail pointed sharply downwards. If disappointed, it will pass on briskly and hover elsewhere, but if it sights a fish near the surface it will aim and plunge, with wings folded, from a height of anything up to ten metres and haul its catch out to a convenient perch, where it batters it to death and consumes it. If the fish is small enough, it will sometimes be eaten on the wing. This bird has a sharp but attractive call which is heard more frequently in flight than at rest.

Finally there is the Common Kingfisher (*Alcedo atthis bengalensis*), the emerald and rust-coloured species which is familiar, although in differing races, not only around Europe but also as far afield as North Africa and Asia through to Australasia. This is seen less frequently at Bharatpur than the two previous species, partly because it is smaller and seems to prefer a greater degree of cover while it perches and waits for its quarry. But it also occasionally hovers and one sees it most often as it flies fast and low from one perch to another, uttering a sharp 'te-tee, te-tee' as it goes.

The kingfishers provide at all times a varied and colourful accompaniment as one walks around the Bharatpur marshes, while, if one is lucky enough, one may see a pair displaying and courting during the early summer. Such is the attractiveness of this bird that one can well understand why, with the nightingale, it has formed a part of mythology since the time of the ancient Greeks. Perhaps the most touching myth is that which relates that the kingfisher was once a rather dull bird, but that when it left Noah's Ark, it flew towards the setting sun; hence its breast was scorched a dull red while its back reflected the blue of the evening sky.

# FOUR 'PERCHERS'

A S I HAVE suggested, it is not possible to do justice to the full
range of Bharatpur's birds without producing a detailed
handbook. However, to fill out a picture of the more prominent and
spectacular species, it seems worthwhile to finish by describing a few
which, although not as sizeable as many of those already reviewed,
nevertheless for one reason or another still manage to catch the eye.
Of these, there is a group which are always much in evidence
because of their method of hunting, which consists of sitting on a
perch with a good view of the surrounding area and then flying
down to take insects or other prey either on the wing or on the
ground. As one moves around the more open areas of Bharatpur,
one cannot fail to pass a succession of 'perchers', each feeding busily
from a vantage point at the centre of its hunting territory.

Of these species, by a long way the most colourful is the Indian
Roller or Blue Jay (*Coracias benghalensis*). In appearance a rather
thick-set bird with a heavy head and beak, it is a strong rather than a
nimble flier and it mostly seeks its prey, which are normally insects
or small mammals, on the ground rather than in the air. When at rest,
it does not present a particularly spectacular sight, its upper parts
being mostly a greenish brown and its breast a reddish buff, while
there is some blue on the head and around the tail and underparts.
The splendour of the bird is only revealed as it flies, when its wings
and tail explode into what every handbook rightly describes as a
splendid combination of Oxford and Cambridge blue. Hugh Whistler
spoke for every birdwatcher in India when he remarked that to the
end of his time in that country, he would never lose the thrill of the
sudden transformation as this 'dark lumpy bird reveals the banded
glory of its wings and tail'. The name 'Roller' derives from the
behaviour of this bird at the start of the breeding season in February,
when its normal sober habits are replaced by a courtship display
which consists of wild twisting dives, zooms and somersaults,
accompanied by harsh screams. At the best of times it is a by no
means silent bird, one of its calls being reminiscent of the twanging
of an out-of-tune guitar. The sound of two Rollers, each twanging on
a different note and both out of tune, is decidedly bizarre.

Another common 'percher', more subdued in colour but

nevertheless both graceful and attractive, is the Little Green Bee-eater (*Merops orientalis*). This is a small, slender bird with a long, slim, slightly decurved beak and long central tail feathers, grass green in colour but tinged with light brown on the head and back. A dark line runs through the eye and another round the upper breast forming a 'gorget'. When in flight, the wings appear almost translucent. Unlike the Roller, the Bee-eater prefers to hunt on the wing, and it launches itself with quick, graceful turns and glides to seize its prey and carry it back to the perch, where it batters it to death before consuming it. Although a solitary hunter, this Bee-eater is also gregarious in habit and a number are not infrequently to be found roosting together, squeezed close along a branch for companionship and warmth. In some places, several hundred may be found in close proximity. Its feet are weak and designed for perching, rather like those of a swift, and it is all but incapable of walking or hopping. It takes itself to the ground only when nesting, the nest being a hole excavated in a bank, which may be up to one-and-a-half metres in length.

A further family of 'perchers', the shrikes, are represented at Bharatpur by several species. Typical of these is the Rufous-backed Shrike (*Lanius schach*), a familiar bird which occurs in several races from the Indian sub-continent through to China. The race found at Bharatpur is the *L. s. erythronotus,* a pale grey bird, reddish-brown on the scapulars and the lower back. A black stripe runs across the forehead and through the eyes, the wings are black, sometimes with

Opposite: *The Blue Jay or Indian Roller* (Coracias benghalensis) *is a common resident of the Indian countryside. It is often seen perched nonchalantly on posts, fences and telegraph wires, and heard far and wide in the breeding season when it performs its noisy and spectacular nuptial aerobatics.*

Top: *The Rufous-backed Shrike* (Lanius schach) *is a common resident, a combative and fiercely territorial bird which eats almost any living creature it can subdue. Like other shrikes, it generally finds a perch sitting upright on a prominent post from where it surveys the terrain for likely prey.*

a small white patch or 'mirror' at the base of the primaries, and the tail is black and brown. The underparts are white tinged with rufous. The Rufous-backed Shrike is more migratory in habit than other species of shrike and, while some individuals appear to be resident in certain areas, the greater number breed in the mountains and in the north-west and west of the sub-continent and move towards peninsular India in the winter. Again, this bird is almost always to be seen on a prominent perch, from which it launches itself on anything of a suitable size which it sees moving on the ground nearby.

There are two prominent characteristics which this shrike shares with other shrike species: the first, which gives it its popular name, 'Butcher Bird', is its practice of maintaining a 'larder' of prey which it has not eaten on the spot but has saved up for later consumption. The 'larder' will consist of a number of insects, small birds and mammals which it has impaled on thorns close together in a convenient tree. The second characteristic is its quite extraordinary powers as a mimic: its normal call is rather harsh, while in the breeding season it has a prolonged, very attractive song, but it can also imitate a wide variety of other birds. Dr Salim Ali gives a list of almost incredible length, including the Pariah Kite, Common and Pied Mynas, House and Yellow-throated Sparrows, swallow, swift, parakeet, Red-vented Bulbul, Common, Jungle and Yellow-eyed Babblers, Grey and Black Partridge, Yellow and Red-wattled Lapwings, Common Sandgrouse, Large and Small Green Bee-eater, Baya, Indian Nightjar, Rain Quail, Large Cuckoo Shrike, Purple Sunbird, Koel, Pied-crested Cuckoo, Hawk-cuckoo, Common and Indian Cuckoos and Magpie-robin. In addition, this shrike is said to have been heard imitating the Striped Squirrel and new-born puppies: it is able to reel off a succession of varying imitations, and is both quick to learn and the possessor of a retentive memory.

Bharatpur's fourth 'percher' is one of India's most ubiquitous and well-known birds, the Drongo or King Crow (*Dicrurus adsimilis albirictus*). This is a graceful, glossy blue-black bird, the distinguishing mark which makes it unmistakable being its deeply forked tail. Like the Bee-eater, the Drongo's build inhibits movement on the ground and it is invariably to be seen either on a suitable vantage point—telegraph posts and wires are a favourite—or hunting from the backs of grazing cattle. Its prey consists wholly of insects, which it takes both on the wing and on the ground and, since it is not above piracy, from other foraging birds. It is a no less pugnacious bird than the shrikes and will attack, fearlessly and noisily, any intruder which threatens its nest. The size of the opponent seems to present no deterrent, and even eagles are not immune from its attack. A Drongo's nest will often have in close proximity the nests of one or more species, such as doves or orioles, who themselves are not at all bellicose, but who have a clear perception of the advantages of a nearby Drongo.

# FOUR
# 'SPECTACULARS'

OTHER BIRDS at Bharatpur catch the eye for no other reason than that they are simply very beautiful. The choice of only four is bound to be invidious, but there is no doubt that pride of place has to be given to the Golden Oriole (*Oriolus oriolus kundoo*), or rather to the male of that species, whose beauty lies not in any great variety of colour, but in a simple combination of body plumage of a dazzling golden yellow and jet black wings and tail. The female is also attractive, greenish-yellow in colour with brown wings and tail and lighter underparts, but for sheer blazing beauty not in the same class as the male.

The oriole is a retiring bird with a dipping flight, often difficult to spot as it moves among the woodland canopy, and its presence is not infrequently revealed, in the summer at least, as much by its mellow call as by the conspicuous colouring of the male. The Indian oriole differs in only minor respects from the European Golden Oriole, one readily noticeable difference being that the small black streak from the lores to the eyes extends behind the eyes in the Indian variety. While the European race occurs as an occasional vagrant as it migrates from Central Asia to Africa, the Indian race is partly resident in the Indian sub-continent (there appear for instance to be a few pairs which spend their whole year at Bharatpur) and partly migratory from the south of the sub-continent to summer breeding areas stretching from Turkestan, Afghanistan, Kashmir and Nepal to northern and north-western India. A pair came regularly to breed in our compound in Delhi, the male for some reason arriving a week to ten days before the female and living in a state of frenzied anticipation until she arrived.

Bharatpur's second immensely beautiful bird is the Paradise Flycatcher (*Terpsiphone paradisi leucogaster*), an aptly named species which also derives its attractiveness from the purity and simplicity of its colouring, enhanced, in the case of the adult male, by a pair of long white streamers which flutter behind him as he flies. He has a metallic blue-black head with a conspicuous crest, while the rest of the plumage is a glistening silvery-white streaked with black. The eye rim and beak are blue. A younger male has a chestnut back and streamers, while the female and first year male have the chestnut

Top: *The beautiful Paradise Flycatcher* (Terpsiphone paradisi) *is a winter visitor to Bharatpur from the Himalayas. Its nest is a compact cup woven from grasses and fibres, plastered on the outside with cobwebs and spiders' egg cases. Both sexes participate in nest-building, incubation and rearing of the young.*

Bottom: *The Golden Oriole* (Oriolus oriolus) *is also known in India as the Mango Bird because of its fondness for groves of leafy trees—in the plains, mango orchards, and, in the hills, Chinar and Sheesham trees. It is chiefly arboreal and prefers to nest in the proximity of the vigilant Drongo.*

106

back and a short tail only. At Bharatpur as elsewhere, these birds are typically to be seen in light woodland, where they lead a restless existence. They are arboreal in habit, perching among the branches and hunting insects tirelessly on the wing. The male appears to be very conscious of the splendour of his tail: he often flits it open while perching and in the breeding season he performs undulating nuptial flights, circling around with slow wingbeats, the tail rising and falling gracefully behind him. In normal flight the fluttering tail tends to obscure his speed and agility, which are more obvious in the females and younger males. If I had to judge the relative beauty of the Golden Oriole and the Paradise Flycatcher, I would find it hard to have to commit mself: the one is glorious, but the other more than compensates through sheer grace of movement and simplicity of colour.

The third 'spectacular' is a much smaller bird, the Red Avadavat (*Estrilda amandava amandava*). This is known throughout India simply by the name of *Lal*—'Red'; it is much sought after as a cage bird and is also exported in large numbers. The name Avadavat is said to be a corruption of Ahmedabad, the former capital of the state of Gujarat, whence these birds were brought over two hundred years ago to the British 'factory' or trading post in Surat. The male in the breeding season is a rich crimson on the body with brown wings, tail and abdomen, and is extensively spotted with white. The female, and

*A female Rose-ringed Parakeet* (Psittacula krameri). *This bird is a resident, widely found in well-watered and wooded tracts. It is highly gregarious and large flocks of parakeets inflict considerable damage every year to farmers and fruit-growers.*

the male outside the breeding season, are also spotted with white, but the female is mostly brownish above, with a little crimson on the tail coverts, and ashy-buff shading to yellow below. Flocks of these lively and attractive little birds are often to be seen around Bharatpur. The area seems to suit them, since they prefer patches of reed or long grass near marshland, while they are also to be found in the surrounding countryside, where clumps of sugarcane are a favourite haunt.

A final bird which is on any reckoning a 'spectacular' is the Rose-ringed Parakeet (*Psittacula krameri borealis*). This bird is found in abundance across most of India, and at Bharatpur its numbers seem to have increased in recent years, along with those of other common species such as doves and mynas. It is a handsome parakeet with bright green plumage with some blue and yellow in it, particularly in the tail. It has a stout red bill and a long pointed tail. The male has a black chin and collar shading into rose-pink on the back of the neck, while the female has an indistinct collar of a slightly brighter green than the rest of the plumage. Pair bonding is strong and the courtship display during the breeding season is conspicuously—almost blatantly—affectionate, with the female appearing to make most of the advances and the male seeming at times almost taken aback at her lack of modesty. At other times these parakeets are highly gregarious and flocks of them cause considerable damage to standing crops. Their flight is strong and fast, and their harsh screams reverberate across the sky as they make their way of an evening to their roosting trees, which they often share with a number of other species. They make their nests in holes of trees, more often preferring to use an existing hole than to make one of their own. The female will spend the greater part of her time in the nest-hole both while incubating her eggs and until the chicks are nearly fully grown, the male bringing food both for her and for their offspring. Like the Avadavat, this parakeet is much in demand in India as a cage bird, and it can become exceedingly tame. It can be taught to speak to a limited extent and is apparently effective with swear words, without, however, being in the same class as, for example, the African Grey Parrot.

# A FINAL FOUR

To CONCLUDE this account of Bharatpur's birds which I have tried to make broadly representative, there are a final four which must be mentioned, partly because they are very much in evidence around the Park and, in one case, illustrative of a whole group of birds, the warblers, for which Bharatpur should be more widely known than it is at present.

The first is the Baya Weaver Bird (*Ploceus philippinus philippinus*), a bird famed for its skill and artistry in building its nests, which are a well-known feature of the Indian countryside. The Baya is a sparrow-sized bird, and both the female and the male outside the breeding season are not unlike a sparrow in appearance and colouring. In the breeding season the male develops a dark mask across the sides of the head and throat, while the crown and breast become bright yellow. This is a gregarious bird, not very obtrusive at Bharatpur during the winter, but very much in evidence any time after April, usually when monsoon conditions begin and with them the breeding season. The Baya builds its nests from strips of grass and similar material, which it weaves into long, retort-shaped structures with an entrance tunnel at the lower end. These nests are attached firmly to the branches of trees, in colonies which may comprise just a handful in number, but may also run into hundreds. Often they are built over water, but it is not unusual, at Bharatpur as elsewhere, to find them in trees in drier areas also, provided that the area is not too heavily wooded. The Baya's mating habits, which are fascinating, commence with frenzied nest construction on the part of the male birds. Young males start building in their first year, but it is clear that the operation is one which needs practice and it is not until their second year that they manage to construct anything which is acceptable for nesting purposes. When the nests are under construction, the females arrive and inspect them, to the accompaniment of a frenzy of invitational display and anticipation on the part of the males. Only if the female finds the nest acceptable does mating take place, after which the nest is finished and the eggs are laid and incubated. This, however, far from satisfies the male's mating instincts and, with energy unabated, he promptly goes off and builds a second nest for a second female, and then a third and

Overleaf: *The Blossom-headed Parakeet* (Psittacula cyanocephala) *is not a regular visitor to Bharatpur, though it is resident in the sub-continent. This specimen, photographed in the garden of the Forest Lodge, must have been a vagrant.*

Top: *The Hoopoe* (Upupa epops) *is a widespread denizen of open woodland and gardens. It is wholly insectivorous and a ground-feeder. The female is entirely responsible for incubation, but the male feeds her dutifully on the nest for the duration.*

Bottom: *A male Baya or Weaver Bird* (Ploceus philippinus). *Bayas are notoriously polygamous and gregarious; they weave their nests in colonies close together, and the distinctive retort-shaped cluster of Baya nests depending from trees or clumps of bushes is a familiar sight all over the Indian countryside.*

perhaps even a fourth. Eventually, however, he runs out of reproductive fervour, when he is liable to leave a nest unfinished and call it a day. So strong is the Baya's gregarious instinct that it is also liable to desert a nest and nestlings if the flock as a whole decides that it is time to leave the nesting colony.

Very occasionally, as Dr Salim Ali has narrated, tame Bayas are to be seen being exhibited around India by itinerant entertainers. It is not surprising, given their weaving skills, that they should have been taught, for example, to thread beads on a pin, but it is altogether more remarkable to see them performing tricks, such as picking out a particular card from a random number, which seem to require some degree of conceptual intelligence. Altogether they are quite remarkable birds, with a pleasantly lively, noisy, gregarious life-style.

Mention must also be made of the minivets, a very colourful group of birds, of which the species which is most commonly seen at Bharatpur is the Small Minivet (*Pericrocotus cinnamomeus peregrinus*). This is a bird which is hardly ever to be seen in open spaces: at Bharatpur its favourite haunt is along those bunds which are flanked with mature trees, and a small party of minivets, generally some eight to twelve in number, is often to be seen progressing methodically along a tree-lined bund, flitting along the branches and among the leaves in search of insects, or hovering to catch them in the air, all along uttering a continuous, rather pleasant low-pitched warbling. The Small Minivet is about the size of a sparrow, but slimmer and with a longer tail. A mature male is black merging to slaty-grey on the head, throat and back, while the wings are similarly coloured, with a small orange patch. In stark contrast, the breast, rump and tips of the tail are a vivid flame-red, while the underparts pale from crimson to yellow and white towards the tail. The female is less brilliantly coloured, lacking the crimson except on the rump and in the tail, the underparts including the throat being a light grey tinged with yellow. Immature males show further variations in colour: commencing with an appearance very similar to that of the female, successive moults progressively replace the grey of the throat and breast with the black and crimson of the adult male. A flock of minivets will thus exhibit an attractive variety of colouring, few being precisely alike. The nest of the Small Minivet is a particularly deft construction, composed of very fine twigs and grass stems bound together with cobwebs and so camouflaged with scraps of bark and moss that it is all but indistinguishable from the branch or fork of the tree to which it is fastened.

The Bharatpur checklist contains over two dozen species of warbler, and yet it seems doubtful if they have been at all comprehensively studied or described: a splendid opportunity would seem to present itself for the production of a definitive work on their status and habits. If I select here only one species of warbler, it is partly because it is one which is very noticeable at Bharatpur, both visually and aurally, and partly because there is no obvious basis for any other selection from among the several species which are commonly to be seen there. The bird which I have selected is the Indian Great Reed Warbler (*Acrocephalus stentoreus brunescens*), a bird which is not dissimilar to the European Great Reed Warbler (*Acrocephalus arundinaceus*), except that it is slightly darker in colour and its call is rather louder. It is a sizeable (18-19 centimetres in length) warbler, olive-brown on the head and back, with a whitish supercilium and with darker brown wings and tail; the chin and throat are white and the underparts buff. This particular race breeds partly in India, but is also a passage migrant in many areas as well as a winter visitor from breeding grounds in Iran and Transcaspia. There is one record in the Journal of the Bombay Natural History Society of a bird ringed near Calcutta in 1965 which was recovered three and a half years later near Samarkand in Uzbekistan, rather more than 2,700 kilometres away.

The reed beds and other dense vegetation around the marshes at Bharatpur provide an ideal habitat for this bird and, while it is occasionally to be seen singing from a perch near the top of a reed, it is often quite possible to approach it closely and to watch it as it moves within its cover. The call has been described as a harsh, guttural 'ke-kee, ke-kee', while the song is also loud and rasping, with a repeated refrain, but also with several variations and pleasing interludes. This warbler also has the reputation of being a mimic, and the distinguished ornithologist Col. Meinertzhagen is said to have been able to distinguish its imitations of the peacock and the bulbul in spring in Afghanistan: he believed, in fact, that it might be possible to tell from the mimicry included in its song where it had spent the previous winter.

Finally, no picture of the birdlife at Bharatpur would be complete without mention of the Hoopoe (*Upupa epops*), a bird which has fascinated mankind since the dawn of recorded history, featuring in myth and literature and being used for magical and even medical purposes. For that reason, and since it is widely distributed throughout Europe, Africa and Asia, a detailed description of this crested, zebra-striped bird with its typical undulating flight would be superfluous. However it has to be recorded that Bharatpur is no exception in presenting, along its tracks and paths and across its open spaces, the frequent sight of one or more Hoopoes pacing methodically to and fro as they probe the ground for the insects and larvae on which they feed. In winter, the resident race *U. e. orientalis* is joined by the slightly larger typical form *U. e. epops*, which migrates to the plains from its breeding grounds in the Himalayas. Hindi is typical of many languages in giving the Hoopoe an onomatopoeic name, in this case *Hūdhūd*.

# A Winter Day's Birdwatching

*The dawn of a winter day in the bird sanctuary at Bharatpur. At this time of year, provided a favourable monsoon has filled the marshes, the Park is one of the most magical places on this earth.*

To TRY TO give some overall concept of the delights of birdwatching at Bharatpur, I have selected from my notes a day in the month of February 1982. A typical winter's day in northern India is warm and sunny, the equivalent of a magnificent, unclouded day at the height of an exceptional British summer, but this day was not typical. There had been heavy rain the day previously and this had caused a build-up of moisture in the atmosphere. The morning therefore dawned in heavy mist, which did not lift for several hours. Thereafter the day remained dull and overcast, with little or no wind, and it was not until well into the afternoon that the sun began to shine fitfully through the clouds.

A dawn start was therefore uninviting, and it was only after breakfast, as the mist began to thin slightly, that I walked down the path behind the Forest Rest House towards the Yashwant Bund. My first companions were a pair of Indian wild boar, whose early appearance was not perhaps as surprising as it may sound, since they have the habit of hanging around the Rest House in the expectation—often fulfilled—of undertaking some successful foraging in the nearby garbage dump. The path ran first through bush and trees, where the silence was broken only occasionally by the parakeets, whose noisy accompaniment was to persist at intervals during the day. After a few hundred yards the marshes began, with an immediate sight of a score or more Purple Moorhens, joined a little further on by a much larger number of Coots. Both species build up at Bharatpur during the winter—the Coots understandably enough since, as I have indicated, they are not only resident in India throughout the year but also migrate from Central Asia for the winter. The Purple Moorhens, however, congregate for no equally apparent reason, since they are residents of the sub-continent. It struck me again how difficult it is to imagine the Coot, with its laboured flight and its wings so apparently small in relation to its dumpy body, undertaking migratory flights across the mountain barrier from Central Asia, but the ringing records are conclusive.

Besides the Coots and moorhens were small groups of Spotbill and Pintail Ducks, the former again resident and the latter migratory, and a few Little Grebes. The latter also seem to multiply in the winter and are only to be seen infrequently at other times of the year. A little further on the marshes open out and it was possible to see for some distance on each side, although on the left the view was to some extent restricted by numbers of small islands planted with *Acacia arabica* . These were the summer nesting sites of many of the storks, egrets, cormorants and the rest, now almost wholly deserted. On a few trees only sat several young Painted Storks, looking rather forsaken and bedraggled in their brown immature plumage. The trees on the right were occupied at this hour by sleeping Darters, their long sinuous necks coiled tightly to their bodies. They could be distinguished from the few cormorants perched with them by their light-coloured heads and the delicate silvery-grey streaks down their backs.

The path now ran along a fully-fledged dyke, the Yashwant Bund, with mature acacia trees on each side. Ahead, a Little Egret stalked across, its yellow feet contrasting with its black legs and bill. On an island to the left stood a Cattle Egret and a motionless Purple Heron, both scanning the water for unwary fish. More Coots and moorhens, this time with the Indian Moorhen joining the larger Purple variety. A few White-breasted Waterhens were paddling in the shallows, together with a single Bronze-winged Jacana. A solitary Glossy Ibis was also wading in the vegetation: surprisingly, there were no White Ibises, which are much the more common species at Bharatpur, visible in the marshes on this side.

Until now I had seen no raptors, but a sudden splashing and commotion far to the right drew attention to perhaps the most magnificent of them all. Some distance in that direction stands a large, solitary, leafless tree supporting in its upper branches a Pallas's Fishing Eagle's nest. I could see through the binoculars the two eagles wheeling and circling: whether their hunt was successful could not be established, but one soon returned to the nest while the other flew over to a tree on the edge of the marsh. Scanning the marsh in the same direction I also picked out two Marsh Harriers, not at this moment wheeling and gliding on the hunt, but one perched on an acacia tree, the other among the reeds.

The marsh at this point broadens out to an expanse of open water. Coots were again in a majority, but were joined here by Red-crested Pochards, some Pintails, a few Tufted Ducks and the odd Shoveler and Gadwall. Towards the far shore was a small group of Greylags, with some more ruminating on the bank. Beyond these was a small group of egrets and Spoonbills, while beyond again was a group of a dozen or so Common Cormorants perched, in Bharatpur fashion, on a leafless tree.

At this point the path reaches the far side of the marsh, and so I retraced my steps. A Grey Heron on my left; more parakeets; and at last the flash of iridescent blue which I had been expecting. This path is the haunt of several White-breasted Kingfishers, and there was one of them perched precariously on a swaying bullrush. Opposite, there was a Dalmatian Pelican floating in solitary state on the far side of the lake, which I had somehow missed on my way out. Back again to the trees and bush, where three Sarus Cranes appeared suddenly on my left, two adults and one young. The young bird was almost fully grown, but still had a brownish head and neck, and was yet to develop the adult colouring. As with many of the other birds, the dull morning seemed to give the cranes confidence and they showed no sign of noticing my presence. Accompanying me on the path at that point were a pair of Hoopoes and a Red-wattled Lapwing, the latter unusually silent and seemingly preoccupied. Normally these birds

Top: *The Spotted Munia*
(Lonchura punctulata) *is a
common and widespread
resident which outside of the
breeding season congregates
in large flocks in the
company of other munias
and weaver birds.*

Bottom: *The Yellow Wagtail*
(Motacilla flava)*, a water-bird
which feeds on insects, larvae
and molluscs, is a winter
visitor from the Caucasian
region.*

are, like blackbirds in Britain, highly irritating, since they can be relied upon to give warning of one's approach to all and sundry at the smallest provocation. Their repeated, piercing cry, 'Did-he-do-it, Did-he-do-it,' seems inevitably to make itself heard at the wrong moment. Finally, as if escorting me back to the Rest House, a magnificent Blue Bull stalked through the trees, a bare twenty metres to my left.

I decided then to try the east side of the Park, towards Nil Tal and Mound Plantation, in the hope of seeing some Siberian Cranes, and so I walked down the central road some way and turned off through the bush to my left. There is a tall tree at this point which is occasionally the perch for one or two White-necked Storks, but today it was occupied by seven White-backed Vultures keeping, as usual, a keen eye open for the dead and dying. As I struck down the edge of the marsh, there, sure enough, were a pair of Siberian Cranes and,

*The Black Partridge* (Francolinus francolinus) *is a resident bird, predominantly ground-dwelling, and found in well-watered areas, usually in scattered pairs or small parties. It is a favourite quarry of sportsmen.*

nearer the shore, three or four flocks of Bar-headed Geese, probably a couple of hundred birds in all. Whether it was the misty morning, or they were simply not in the mood to be bothered, the geese were, like the Sarus Cranes earlier, not their usual uptight selves. I was careful not to approach too close, but for once they seemed determined not to be disturbed. I was able to note what seems to be an established difference of habit between the Greylags and the Bar-headed: whereas the former seem to be quite contented just sitting, standing or floating around during the day, the latter seemed to prefer the muddy verges of the marsh, where they forage for food. The handbooks say that the Bar-headed are crepuscular or nocturnal feeders and that they snooze out of harm's way during the day: here at Bharatpur they seem to occupy their days with some assiduous feeding, while it is the Greylag who seem content in day-time to do nothing in particular, nowhere in particular.

Then—the next thrill of the day—perched on a tree at the edge of the marsh was a Lesser Spotted Eagle. It was possible to approach quite close and to see very clearly the two rows of white markings on the wings, indicating that it was an immature bird and, because the markings were not more extensive, that it was of the Lesser Spotted species. When it eventually flew, its dull white patch became visible on the rump and the under-wing coverts showed lighter than the primaries.

The weather was still dull as I skirted the end of the Jatoli Canal and walked down the eastern side of Mound Plantation. My immediate objective was the other Pallas's Fishing Eagle's nest, which some weeks earlier I had been able to photograph from a tower hide. This time, life had moved on and one of the adults was on the nest with two offspring, while the other was perched on a tree on the far shore. The guard was changed while I was there: the young subsided, evidently having been fed, and the adult departed. Simultaneously the other adult flew in and took up station on a tree-top close by.

The walk down the remaining length of this marsh was notable mainly for the waterfowl. Both Greylag and Bar-headed Geese, the former again on the marsh, the latter feeding on the verge. More Pintail, but Common Teal and Common Pochard with them (and more Coots). Across the marsh, where they seem to have a popular resting place, a line of Spoonbills on a low bank; and, at the end, a solitary, lugubrious-looking Black-necked Stork. A few hundred metres into the bush to the east of the marsh at this point, a pair of these birds have their nest at the top of a high acacia tree: judging from the yellow eye, this was the female of the pair.

Along the path, my eye was caught by a quick flutter from a wayside bush. The bush was thick and its inhabitant more than usually elusive. However, when I did at last get a clear view, it presented no difficulty. A chestnut breast and a quiver of white in the tail proclaimed a Red-breasted Flycatcher, India's nearest equivalent to the British Robin.

My next objective was one of the southern marshes, in the hope of seeing some more Siberian Cranes. In this I was not disappointed, since seven of them were there, not one hundred metres from the dyke. I took my lunch quietly, half hidden by a bush, and watched them for a time. They were not at that moment feeding: rather they were preening or, if not preening, quietly gazing into the middle distance. After half an hour or so, three of them—two adults and a young bird—flew off some distance where I later saw them feeding. The other two pairs remained and continued to preen. Through the binoculars I could admire once again the beauty of these birds—the snow-white plumage, the contrast of the pinkish-red face and legs, the long feathers drooping at the tail. There was no hint of the black of their outer flight feathers as they stood, but the black and white contrast when they flew was nothing less than dazzling. At one moment, one pair took it into their heads to trumpet, for no apparent reason. They nodded their heads up and down quite rapidly, emitting the cry when the head was stretched vertically upwards.

The Siberian Cranes were not the only lunch-time diversion. As usual, I was alerted to the presence of a Marsh Harrier first by the flurry of a flock of Coots and ducks half-way across the marsh. I then saw the Harrier gliding low beneath the tree line and swooping on the various groups of waterfowl, which concentrated for safety. This went on intermittently for some time; and it was only after retracing my steps a little while later that I saw the upshot—the contented Harrier on a low bank in the marsh pecking at its kill. Incredibly, a flock of Pintail, Cotton Teal and Common Teal paddled around nearby quite unconcerned, either realising that the Harrier was well sated for the time being or, more probably, not sensing danger while the Harrier was not on the wing. I then realised that there had been, as is not uncommon, two Harriers, as the second of the pair emerged from behind the nearby trees, still gliding low across the marsh.

This area of the Park seems to be a favourite ground for the Greylag, and over a hundred of them were standing or floating around a short distance away. Small groups occasionally flew off and other small groups flew in, again for no apparent reason, but making a good deal of fuss about it. Geese, at least at Bharatpur, seem incapable of being silent except when more or less immobile—movement is always accompanied by noise. In the trees along this part of the dyke were also a few thrills: a pair of Red-breasted Woodpeckers tapping at the bark and, sharing a bush overlooking the marsh, a Common Kingfisher and a Bay-backed Shrike, the former fishing and the latter on the look-out for insects on the wing. Below the path was the flick of a chestnut tail and there was a Bluethroat. 'Bluethroat' is really a misnomer for this lovely bird: the colouring on the throat is variable, but on this occasion it was

Overleaf: *The Purple Sunbird* (Nectarina asiatica) *is a common and widespread resident, often to be seen flitting and hopping through foliage, using its specially adapted bill and tongue to sip nectar from flowers. Its nest is an untidy pouch woven from grass and fibres, leaves, bark and cobwebs.*

Top: *The Small Green Bee-eater* (Merops orientalis) *is a resident, usually found in flocks of 15-20. Bee-eaters are often called Rainbow Birds on account of their brilliant colouring. They are agile and expert fliers and catch insects on the wing as well as on the ground.* [See pg. 103]

Bottom: *The Grey Shrike* (Lanius excubitor), *a resident of the carnivorous Butcher Bird family, is a bold and aggressive bird which in Mughal times was trained along with falconets to hunt sparrows and small game birds.*

banded, in order downwards, blue, dark blue, chestnut, blue, dark blue, white and chestnut, a display which seemed somewhat out of place against the subdued colouring of the rest of the bird.

I retraced my steps the way I had come. Much was as before, but somehow three pairs of Sarus Cranes had materialised close to the path. Also there was a White-tailed Lapwing: not unlike the Red-wattled Lapwing in manner, except that it seems to be fairly quiet and is normally to be found only near water. It is also much less conspicuous in colouring, mostly light brown with a greyish breast, white underparts and yellow legs. It is a not very common winter migrant from Central Asia.

Back towards the Fishing Eagles' nest the path runs under some electricity cables leading to one of the tube wells installed to keep the Park alive in 1979. Huddled tightly together on one of the wires were six Little Green Bee-eaters, evidently still feeling the chill of the day, while out along the wire were a number of swallows, both Common and Wire-tailed. A little further along, a flash of red and gold revealed the presence of a Golden-backed Woodpecker, and its mate also quickly materialised in a neighbouring tree. Yet further along, a flurry in the muddy verges of the marsh drew my attention to two small waders. One flashed a white rump and I was able to identify a Spotted Sandpiper. The other showed no white and indeed while at rest was all but impossible to see among the grass. It took some minutes of watching to identify it as a Snipe, so effective was the camouflage. A little further on I was reassured on the subject of pelicans, having seen only the one Dalmatian. Eleven Rosy Pelicans were soaring high over the marsh, in company with four Painted Storks.

The path back beside the eastern marsh revealed no new surprises apart from a startled hare, and so I thought that I would continue through the bush into Nil Tal before rejoining the road. This was rewarding, as I came across one of those congregations of birds which seem to appear suddenly in the middle of apparently bird-deserted territory. There were some Pied Mynas, a Hoopoe or two, a Roller and a few Bush Shrikes. Then, flitting through the bushes, a White-browed Fantail Flycatcher: the conspicuous white streak across the head and its habit of spreading its white-tipped tail made it easy to pick out. In another nearby bush was an even more attractive bird: greenish-yellow above and bright yellow below, with white-barred wings and tail, this was an Iora.

For a final leg, I decided to strike across the road and prospect the Nauka Vihar marsh. A raised path runs out into the marshes here, leading to a hide, and this was the setting for the final delight of the day: on a dead tree near the hide was a Crested Serpent Eagle. Through the binoculars, the black and white crest, although not raised, was clearly visible, as were the ocellations on the body feathers.

Finally, the path along the shore back to the Rest House was not wholly without interest: a Drongo and a Bay-backed Shrike in the bushes along the verge, and overhead a hundred or more Painted Storks soaring in the late afternoon light. Also a jackal, an encounter which gave me a touch of pleasure since it was I who saw him, while he did not see me.

This was not an exceptional day: if anything the dull light made it a little disappointing. I have transposed from my notes only the more exciting sightings and have omitted many of the more commonplace, the babblers, bulbuls, robins, doves and so on. This chapter nevertheless mentions some sixty species of bird—not an out-of-the-way number; and a more experienced Bharatpur hand would probably have spotted many more. Yet I hope that it does go some way towards illustrating the wealth and variety of Bharatpur's birdlife. The veteran ornithologist H.G. Alexander records (in *Seventy Years of Birdwatching*) that he compiled a list of over one hundred birds at Bharatpur in the course of a two-day outing from Delhi, which would not have given him much more than a full day actually in the Park. This is perhaps some measure of the interest and enjoyment which Bharatpur can provide even for the passing visitor.

# THE FUTURE

*Grey Heron in flight over the marshes. With the mounting pressures of growing population and rapid industrialization, sanctuaries like Bharatpur are all that remain of India's former extensive wetlands, and this too, lives uneasily under threat.*

127

I T SEEMS right to conclude with some thoughts about the future of Bharatpur, partly since it is in global terms such an important and valuable wildlife reserve, and partly because some of the issues raised have a more general conservation relevance.

Until not much more than a generation ago, Bharatpur was a part of a much larger wilderness, and it was possible for wild animals to move in and out of the Park from surrounding areas of forest and bush. With the spread of irrigation and the growth of population, these surrounding areas have become increasingly cultivated and Bharatpur is now a besieged enclave. Until recently, the pressures had seemed to be irresistible and it appeared to be only a matter of time before the Park would be effectively destroyed as a bird and wildlife sanctuary. While the Maharaja had traditionally permitted a limited number of cattle from the neighbouring villages to graze in the Park, control had been virtually lost and thousands of cattle and buffaloes had been allowed to wander at will. Wood-gatherers were active and poaching not infrequent. On any weekend or holiday, the road through the centre of the Park would be thronged with buses, cars and tongas, as transistor-carrying picnickers came to enjoy the amenities of the only area of natural countryside which now exists for many miles around. The consequence of all these activities was a harassment of the Park's wildlife and a progressive degradation of its environment which was all too obvious to anyone who had visited Bharatpur over a period of time.

This was all well documented in a report drawn up by the Tourism and Wildlife Society of India in 1981, which pointed out that perhaps a quarter of the trees at Bharatpur had disappeared in the previous four years. Areas which had been heavily wooded and thick with undergrowth had assumed the appearance of open savannah. The grass was being eaten to its roots over wide areas, while others had turned to dust under the hooves of the cattle as they were herded to and from the villages to which they belonged. The number of nesting Sarus Cranes had greatly diminished, as had those of many of the migrant or locally migrant species, notably the cranes, pelicans, geese and ducks. Nesting birds had been disturbed in the marshes by the wading buffaloes and the fish suffocated by their stirring up of sand and mud. Of the mammals, the last leopard had been killed about a decade previously, while the numbers of Cheetal and Black Buck had decreased spectacularly.

In November 1982, however, matters were brought to a head, with the result that control was reestablished and an effective stop was put to the entry and grazing of cattle and buffaloes. The wall which had been built around the Park, which had not been completed and which had been breached in places, was repaired and its completion put in hand. Control was exercised over the movement of vehicles in the Park and their numbers greatly reduced. Immediate benefits were seen and more can undoubtedly follow: the deer, which had clearly been discouraged by the presence of so many cattle, were suddenly again very much in evidence, while the migrant geese seemed much more settled and willing to remain in the Park in larger numbers. If all goes well, there is every likelihood of a revival of vegetation and undergrowth, and with it an encouragement of the nesting activities of many of the resident species. In the longer term, the heavier vegetation will also undoubtedly benefit.

It is nevertheless too early to say whether this improvement will last. As elsewhere, there is a human dimension here to the question of wildlife preservation, and one which gives rise to a genuine dilemma. The problem is somewhat different from those with which we are faced in the Western world. Here, our wildlife is being destroyed through the consequences of affluence. Our forests and lakes are being killed by the fall-out from the fossil fuels used by industry and transport systems; our woods and wetlands are being cleared and drained for the benefit of agro-business; our countryside is being increasingly ravaged by pesticides, herbicides, artificial fertilisers and prairie farming methods on the one hand and by the spread of urbanisation on the other. Even our most remote areas—the Western Isles of Scotland are the latest to be threatened—seem not to be immune. Only with difficulty do we establish limited areas in which some semblance of the natural order can be preserved. In a country like India, on the other hand, the problems are those of poverty, rather than of affluence; but they are no less difficult for that. I am reminded of being told some years ago by a Wildlife Officer in Tanzania of the incomprehension of tribesmen living on the margins of the Serengeti Plain at their being forbidden to kill animals for food, while scientists in the Park were freely shooting zebras in order to analyse their infestation by internal parasites. Bharatpur is now surrounded by villages and is close to a sizeable town. The poverty of the Indian villager is acute and the pressures on him harsh, to an extent which can hardly be appreciated by a Westerner. His cattle, unproductive and poor in quality as they often are, are both a measure of wealth and some guarantee against destitution. To provide himself with warmth and cooking fuel, he must rely not only on dried dung from his cattle, but also on firewood, since he cannot easily afford more expensive alternatives. Furthermore his numbers are inexorably growing and the mouths which have to be fed more numerous as the years go by. He too does not understand why his real and pressing needs should be subordinated to the preservation of wildlife.

The extremes and unpredictability of the Indian climate are a further cause for concern. Following the drought of 1979-80, which caused grave damage to the Park and its wildlife, a study was made which produced some interesting conclusions. It found that the lack of rainfall caused both an imbalance in, and a reduction in the diversity of, the natural ecosystem of the Park. Plant communities

*Aerial view of Bharatpur showing the medieval town, newer settlements around it, villages beyond and the Keoladeo Ghana National Park.*

were destroyed and organisms at higher trophic levels correspondingly affected. There was a considerable reduction in the numbers of nesting and water birds, in terms both of species and of individuals. A mass migration of many nesting birds took place, to neighbouring areas, and the numbers of migrant waterfowl were reduced to between a fifth and a third of the original populations. The birds which remained were more crowded, were more disturbed by cattle, which also gravitated to the residual pools of water, and were more vulnerable to attack from predators. Land birds such as mynas, babblers and shrikes, on the other hand, benefited, resulting in what seems to be a permanent increase in these and other dry land species.

Waders also increased in numbers in 1979, reflecting the growth in area of the mud flats and shallow waters by which they are attracted. However, while Bharatpur has a variety of waders on its checklist, the

habitat, except in relatively few areas, is by no means ideal for them. These species are therefore normally never seen in the Park in numbers comparable to those which are commonplace on the Jamuna river, not many miles away, still less to those of the huge migratory flocks which are to be found on suitable sites along the east coast of India. The increase in the number of waders at Bharatpur during 1979-80 has thus not been maintained.

The effects of the drought of 1979 have been compounded by another more serious one in 1987, less than a decade later. Again, there seems to have been a wholesale loss of breeding species and water birds. After 1979, a considerable recovery took place, not least on the part of many of the nesting species. On the other hand, there was also a discernible shift in favour of what one may call the species of lower conservation value. The Siberian Cranes, for example, were badly affected. To what extent the Park will manage to survive the most recent catastrophe can only be a matter of conjecture. The effects of the droughts at Bharatpur can be mitigated only marginally by pumping up groundwater and the survival of many of the Park's most interesting species can only be said to be in the lap of the gods.

Especially since Bharatpur's marshlands are mainly man-made, management is also a vital element in the future of the Park; in particular, maintenance of the bunds, canals and sluices which are essential to its survival, as also the control of weeds such as the water hyacinth which, if left undisturbed, would choke the lakes within the space of a few years. A threat which has become apparent in the past few years, perhaps as a consequence of the exclusion of the water buffalo, is the spread of the marsh grass *Paspalum distichon*, which is threatening to choke formerly open stretches of water and to discourage the use of Bharatpur by ducks as their winter feeding area. A general problem is that there are still too many unanswered questions about Bharatpur's eco-system. The Bombay Natural History Society has sponsored a five-year programme, as part of an India-wide Avifauna Project, which is designed to study such aspects as the chemical composition of the water in the marshes, the flora and fauna of the marshland, the feeding habits of some of the nesting species, the patterns of migration and so on. This is an encouraging development, although it is too soon to say what findings the researchers will produce and whether they will point to any deleterious trends which might be remedied by managerial action.

Hardly less important is the preservation and renewal of the forest areas. Much planting has been done, particularly of *Acacia nilotica,* to increase the sites available for the summer nesting species, but the battle has, on balance, been a losing one in recent years. Also vital is the protection of the dry areas against the risk of fire, which becomes particularly acute towards the end of the dry season. There is a fascinating aspect to this problem in the shape of the one traditional industry which used to exist in the Park, the distilling of perfume from Khās, the tall pampas-like grass which flourishes in its southern areas in particular. This industry, which featured at Bharatpur for at least a century, was revived each year with the grant of contracts first to cut the grass, the stems of which are used as thatch, and then to dig up the roots from which the perfume is derived. The roots are chopped up and then simmered with water in a number of stills, condensing out the essential oil into separate closed containers. The resulting perfume is strong and valuable. The last time that the contract was granted, in 1981, it was worth Rs 1,50,000—not far short of £7,500—to the Forests Department. However, the regulations governing National Parks precluded the granting of a contract in 1982, and the Khās, which spreads through its roots, has consequently become rampant and a progressively more serious fire hazard.

There is, additionally, the problem of the feral cattle which roam the Park. There were some 400 of these in the mid-1980s, and their numbers have probably been growing since at a rate of some 100 each year. There is clearly a problem building up here, if no control measures are taken. One method might be to reintroduce a small number of predators, say leopards, which would not only control the feral cattle but would also very probably improve the quality of the herds of deer by culling the weaker or defective specimens. However, the close proximity of a number of villages would seem to rule out such a solution for all practical purposes.

These are some of the problems which affect the management and preservation of the Bharatpur National Park. It is of course easier to expound them than to find solutions which are both practical and humane. But it is encouraging to know that India is in the forefront of the movement for wildlife preservation, for which its leaders have, over the years, shown an enlightened concern. That India has been prepared, albeit late in the day, to devote considerable resources to the splendidly successful campaign to save the Indian tiger gives cause for optimism. I personally am impressed by the metaphor of the canary in the coal-mine. If we cannot preserve our natural heritage, even in enclaves of the interest and importance of Bharatpur, it is unlikely that the world will long remain a place in which the human species can itself survive. Bharatpur, perhaps the finest of Asia's bird sanctuaries, must surely be saved for posterity.

# BIBLIOGRAPHY

## Books about Indian Birds

*A Synopsis of the Birds of India and Pakistan* by S. Dillon Ripley
Bombay Natural History Society, Bombay, 1961
*Handbook of the Birds of India and Pakistan* (vols. 1-10)
by Salim Ali & S. Dillon Ripley, Oxford University Press, Bombay, 1968-1974
*The Book of Indian Birds* by Salim Ali, Bombay Natural History Society, Bombay, 1979
*Indian Hill Birds* by Salim Ali, Oxford University Press, Bombay, 1979
*Collins Handguide to the Birds of the Indian Subcontinent* by Martin Woodcock
Collins, London, 1980
*Popular Handbook of Indian Birds* by Hugh Whistler, Oliver and Boyd, 1963
*A Guide to the Birds of the Delhi Area* by Usha Ganguli
Indian Council for Agricultural Research, New Delhi, 1975
*A Study of the Flora and Fauna of Bharatpur Bird Sanctuary* by V.S. Saxena
Department of Tourism, Govt. of Rajasthan, 1975

## Books of General Interest to the Birdwatcher at Bharatpur

*The Birds of the Palearctic Fauna: A Systematic Reference* by Charles Vaurie
H.F. and G. Witherby, London, 1959-1965
*An Atlas of the Birds of the Western Palearctic* by Colin Harrison, Collins, London, 1982
*Bird Migration* by Chris Mead, Country Life Books, Feltham, England, 1983
*The Birds of the Wetlands* by James Hancock, Croom Helm, London, 1984
*Herons of the World* by J. Hancock and H. Elliott, Harper and Row, New York, 1978
*Wading Birds of the World* by Eric and Richard Soothill, Blandford, Poole, England, 1982
*Wild Geese* by M.A. Ogilvie, T. and A.D. Poyser, Berkhampsted, England, 1978
*Wildfowl of the World,* by Eric Soothill and Peter Whitehead, Blandford, Poole, England, 1978
*The Waterfowl of the World* (vols. 1-4), by J. Delacour, Country Life, London, 1954-64
*Birds of Prey of the World* by M.L. Grossman and J. Hamlet, Cassell, London, 1965
*Cranes of the World* by Lawrence H. Walkinshaw, Winchester Press, New York, 1973
*Owls of the World* by J.A. Burton, Peter Lowe, Weert, 1973

# APPENDIX
## Checklist of the Birds of Bharatpur

### PODICIPITIFORMES

| | |
|---|---|
| **Grebes** | *Podicipedidae* |
| Great Crested Grebe | *Podiceps cristatus* |
| Black-necked Grebe | *Podiceps nigricollis* |
| Dabchick or Little Grebe | *Tachybaptus ruficollis* |

### PELECANIFORMES

| | |
|---|---|
| **Pelicans** | *Pelecanidae* |
| Rosy Pelican | *Pelecanus onocrotalus* |
| Grey or Spot-billed Pelican | *Pelecanus philippensis* |
| Dalmatian Pelican | *Pelecanus crispus* |
| **Cormorants** | *Phalacrocoracidae* |
| Large Cormorant | *Phalacrocorax carbo* |
| Indian Shag | *Phalacrocorax fuscicollis* |
| Little Cormorant | *Phalacrocorax niger* |
| **Darters** | *Anhingidae* |
| Indian Darter | *Anhinga rufa melanogaster* |

### CICONIIFORMES

| | |
|---|---|
| **Herons, Egrets, Bitterns** | *Ardeidae* |
| Grey Heron | *Ardea cinerea* |
| Purple Heron | *Ardea purpurea* |
| Pond Heron | *Ardeola grayii* |
| Cattle Egret | *Bubulcus ibis* |
| Large Egret | *Egretta alba* |
| Median Egret | *Egretta intermedia* |
| Little Egret | *Egretta garzetta* |
| Night Heron | *Nycticorax nycticorax* |
| Chestnut Bittern | *Ixobrychus cinnamomeus* |
| Black Bittern | *Dupetor flavicollis* |
| Bittern | *Botaurus stellaris* |
| **Storks** | *Ciconiidae* |
| Painted Stork | *Mycteria leucocephalus* |
| Openbill Stork | *Anastomus oscitans* |
| White-necked Stork | *Ciconia episcopus* |
| White Stork | *Ciconia ciconia* |

| | |
|---|---|
| Black-necked Stork | *Ephippiorhynchus asiaticus* |
| Adjutant Stork | *Leptoptilos dubius* |
| Lesser Adjutant Stork | *Leptoptilos javanicus* |
| **Ibises, Spoonbills** | ***Threskiornithidae*** |
| White Ibis | *Threskiornis melanocephala* |
| Black Ibis | *Pseudibis papillosa* |
| Glossy Ibis | *Plegadis falcinellus* |
| Spoonbill | *Platalea leucorodia* |
| **Flamingoes** | ***Phoenicopteridae*** |
| Greater Flamingo | *Phoenicopterus roseus* |

## ANSERIFORMES

| | |
|---|---|
| **Geese, Ducks** | ***Anatidae*** |
| Greylag Goose | *Anser anser* |
| White-fronted Goose | *Anser albifrons* |
| Bar-headed Goose | *Anser indicus* |
| Ruddy Shelduck or Brahminy Duck | *Tadorna ferruginea* |
| Common Shelduck | *Tadorna tadorna* |
| Lesser Whistling Teal | *Dendrocygna javanica* |
| Marbled Teal | *Marmaronetta angustirostris* |
| Pintail | *Anas acuta* |
| Common Teal | *Anas crecca* |
| Spotbill | *Anas poecilorhyncha* |
| Mallard | *Anas platyrhynchos* |
| Gadwall | *Anas strepera* |
| Falcated Teal | *Anas falcata* |
| Wigeon | *Anas penelope* |
| Garganey or Blue-winged Teal | *Anas querquedela* |
| Shoveler | *Anas clypeata* |
| Red-crested Pochard | *Netta rufina* |
| Common Pochard | *Aythya ferina* |
| White-eyed Pochard | *Aythya nyroca* |
| Tufted Duck | *Aythya fuligula* |
| Cotton Teal or Pygmy Goose | *Nettapus coromandelianus* |
| Comb Duck | *Sarkidiornis melanotus* |

## FALCONIFORMES

| | |
|---|---|
| **Birds of Prey, Vultures** | ***Accipitridae*** |
| Black-winged Kite | *Elanus caeruleus* |
| Honey Buzzard | *Pernis ptilorhynchus* |
| Pariah or Black Kite | *Milvus migrans* |
| Brahminy Kite | *Haliastur indus* |
| Goshawk | *Accipiter gentilis* |
| Shikra | *Accipiter badius* |
| Sparrowhawk | *Accipiter nisus* |
| Besra Sparrowhawk | *Accipiter virgatus* |
| Long-legged Buzzard | *Buteo rufinus* |
| Desert Buzzard | *Buteo vulpinus* |
| White-eyed Buzzard-Eagle | *Butaster teesa* |
| Bonelli's Hawk-Eagle | *Hieraaetus fasciatus* |

| | |
|---|---|
| Booted Hawk-Eagle | *Hieraaetus pennatus* |
| Golden Eagle | *Aquila chrysaetos* |
| Imperial Eagle | *Aquila heliaca* |
| Tawny Eagle | *Aquila rapax* |
| Steppe Eagle | *Aquila nipalensis* |
| Greater Spotted Eagle | *Aquila clanga* |
| Lesser Spotted Eagle | *Aquila pomarina* |
| White-tailed Sea Eagle | *Haliaeetus albicilla* |
| Ring-tailed or Pallas's Fishing Eagle | *Haliaeetus leucoryphus* |
| Black or Pondicherry Vulture | *Torgus calvus* |
| Indian Long-billed Vulture | *Gyps indicus* |
| Indian White-backed Vulture | *Gyps bengalensis* |
| Egyptian Vulture | *Neophron percnopterus* |
| Hen Harrier | *Circus cyaneus* |
| Pallid Harrier | *Circus macrourus* |
| Montagu's Harrier | *Circus pygargus* |
| Pied Harrier | *Circus melanoleucos* |
| Marsh Harrier | *Circus aeruginosus* |
| Short-toed Eagle | *Circaetus gallicus* |
| Crested Serpent Eagle | *Spilornis cheela* |
| **Osprey** | ***Pandionidae*** |
| Osprey | *Pandion haliaetus* |
| **Falcons** | ***Falconidae*** |
| Saker Falcon | *Falco biarmicus cherrug* |
| Laggar Falcon | *Falco biarmicus jugger* |
| Peregrine Falcon | *Falco peregrinus* |
| Hobby | *Falco subbuteo* |
| Oriental Hobby | *Falco severus* |
| Kestrel | *Falco tinnunculus* |

## GALLIFORMES

| | |
|---|---|
| **Partridges, Quails, Peafowl** | ***Phasianidae*** |
| Black Partridge | *Francolinus francolinus* |
| Grey Partridge | *Francolinus pondicerianus* |
| Common Quail | *Coturnix coturnix* |
| Jungle Bush Quail | *Perdicula asiatica* |
| Common Peafowl | *Pavo cristatus* |

## GRUIFORMES

| | |
|---|---|
| **Bustard-Quails** | ***Turnicidae*** |
| Common Bustard-Quail | *Turnix suscitator* |
| **Cranes** | ***Gruidae*** |
| Common Crane | *Grus grus* |
| Sarus Crane | *Grus antigone* |
| Siberian or Great White Crane | *Grus leucogeranus* |
| Demoiselle Crane | *Anthropoides virgo* |
| **Rails, Crakes, Coots** | ***Rallidae*** |
| Water Rail | *Rallus aquaticus* |
| Baillon's Crake | *Porzana pusilla* |
| Spotted Crake | *Porzana porzana* |
| Ruddy Crake | *Amaurornis fuscus* |

| | |
|---|---|
| Brown Crake | *Amaurornis akool* |
| White-breasted Waterhen | *Amaurornis phoenicurus* |
| Water Cock | *Gallicrex cinerea* |
| Indian Moorhen | *Gallinula chloropus* |
| Purple Moorhen | *Porphyrio porphyrio* |
| Coot | *Fulica atra* |

## CHARADRIIFORMES

| | |
|---|---|
| **Jacanas** | ***Jacanidae*** |
| Pheasant-tailed Jacana | *Hydrophasianus chirugus* |
| Bronze-winged Jacana | *Metopidius indicus* |
| **Snipe** | ***Rostratulidae*** |
| Painted Snipe | *Rostratula benghalensis* |
| **Plovers** | ***Charadriidae*** |
| White-tailed Lapwing | *Vanellus leucurus* |
| Sociable Lapwing | *Vanellus gregarius* |
| Lapwing, Peewit | *Vanellus vanellus* |
| Grey-headed Lapwing | *Vanellus cinereus* |
| Red-wattled Lapwing | *Vanellus indicus* |
| Spur-winged Plover | *Vanellus spinosus* |
| Yellow-wattled Lapwing | *Vanellus malabaricus* |
| Grey Plover | *Pluvialis squatarola* |
| Eastern Golden Plover | *Pluvialis dominica* |
| Eastern Ringed Plover | *Charadrius hiaticula* |
| Little Ringed Plover | *Charadrius dubius* |
| Kentish Plover | *Charadrius alexandrinus* |
| Lesser Sand Plover | *Charadrius mongolus* |
| **Sandpipers** | ***Scolopacidae*** |
| Curlew | *Numenius arquata* |
| Black-tailed Godwit | *Limosa limosa* |
| Spotted or Dusky Redshank | *Tringa erythropus* |
| Common Redshank | *Tringa totanus* |
| Marsh Sandpiper | *Tringa stagnatilis* |
| Greenshank | *Tringa nebularia* |
| Green Sandpiper | *Tringa ochropus* |
| Wood Sandpiper | *Tringa glareola* |
| Terek Sandpiper | *Xenus cinereus* |
| Common Sandpiper | *Actitis hypoleucos* |
| Turnstone | *Arenaria interpres* |
| Pintail Snipe | *Gallinago stenura* |
| Fantail Snipe | *Gallinago gallinago* |
| Jack Snipe | *Lymnocryptes minimus* |
| Knot | *Calidris canutus* |
| Little Stint | *Calidris minutus* |
| Temminck's Stint | *Calidris temminckii* |
| Dunlin | *Calidris alpinus* |
| Curlew-Sandpiper | *Calidris testaceus* |
| Broad-billed Sandpiper | *Limicola falcinellus* |
| Ruff | *Philomachus pugnax* |
| **Phalaropes** | ***Phalaropodidae*** |
| Red-necked Phalarope | *Phalaropus lobatus* |

| | |
|---|---|
| **Stilts, Avocets** | *Recurvirostridae* |
| Black-winged Stilt | *Himantopus himantopus* |
| Avocet | *Recurvirostra avosetta* |
| **Thick-Knees** | *Burhinidae* |
| Stone Curlew | *Burhinus oedicnemus* |
| **Coursers, Pratincoles** | *Glareolidae* |
| Indian Courser | *Cursorius coromandelicus* |
| Collared Pratincole | *Glareola pratincola* |
| Small Indian Pratincole | *Glareola lactea* |
| **Gulls, Terns** | *Laridae* |
| Herring Gull | *Larus argentatus* |
| Great Black-headed Gull | *Larus ichthyaetus* |
| Brown-headed Gull | *Larus brunnicephalus* |
| Whiskered Tern | *Chlidonias hybridus* |
| Black Tern | *Chlidonias niger* |
| Gull-billed Tern | *Gelochelidon nilotica* |
| Caspian Tern | *Hydroprogne caspia* |
| Indian River Tern | *Sterna aurantia* |
| Common Tern | *Sterna hirundo* |
| Black-bellied Tern | *Sterna melanogaster* |
| Little Tern | *Sterna albifrons* |
| Indian Skimmer | *Rynchops albicollis* |

## COLUMBIFORMES

| | |
|---|---|
| **Sandgrouse** | *Pteroclididae* |
| Indian Sandgrouse | *Pterocles exustus* |
| Imperial Sandgrouse | *Pterocles orientalis* |
| **Pigeons, Doves** | *Columbidae* |
| Green Pigeon | *Treron phoenicoptera* |
| Blue Rock Pigeon | *Columba livia* |
| Eastern Stock Pigeon | *Columba eversmanni* |
| Rufous Turtle Dove | *Streptopelia orientalis* |
| Indian Ring Dove | *Streptopelia decaocto* |
| Red Turtle Dove | *Streptopelia tranquebarica* |
| Spotted Dove | *Streptopelia chinensis* |
| Little Brown Dove | *Streptopelia senegalensis* |

## PSITTACIFORMES

| | |
|---|---|
| **Parakeets** | *Psittacidae* |
| Rose-ringed Parakeet | *Psittacula krameri* |

## CUCULIFORMES

| | |
|---|---|
| **Cuckoos, Crow Pheasants** | *Cuculidae* |
| Pied Crested Cuckoo | *Clamator jacobinus* |
| Hawk-Cuckoo, Brain-fever Bird | *Cuculus varius* |
| Indian Plaintive Cuckoo | *Cacomantis passerinus* |
| Koel | *Eudynamys scolopacea* |
| Sirkeer Cuckoo | *Taccocua leschenaultii* |
| Crow-Pheasant, Coucal | *Centropus sinensis* |

# STRIGIFORMES

| **Owls** | *Strigidae* |
|---|---|
| Scops Owl | *Otus scops* |
| Collared Scops Owl | *Otus bakkamoena* |
| Great Horned or Eagle-Owl | *Bubo bubo* |
| Dusky Horned Owl | *Bubo coromandus* |
| Brown Fish Owl | *Bubo ceylonensis* |
| Brown Hawk Owl | *Ninox scutulata* |
| Spotted Owlet | *Athene brama* |
| Mottled Wood Owl | *Strix ocellata* |
| Short-eared Owl | *Asio flammeus* |

# CAPRIMULGIFORMES

| **Nightjars** | *Caprimulgidae* |
|---|---|
| Indian Jungle Nightjar | *Caprimulgus indicus* |
| Syke's Nightjar | *Caprimulgus mahrattensis* |
| Common Indian Nightjar | *Caprimulgus asiaticus* |
| Franklin's Nightjar | *Caprimulgus affinis* |

# APODIFORMES

| **Swifts** | *Apodidae* |
|---|---|
| Alpine Swift | *Apus melba* |
| House Swift | *Apus affinis* |
| Palm Swift | *Cypsiurus parvus* |

# CORACIIFORMES

| **Kingfishers** | *Alcedinidae* |
|---|---|
| Lesser Pied Kingfisher | *Ceryle rudis* |
| Common Kingfisher | *Alcedo atthis* |
| Stork-billed Kingfisher | *Pelargopsis capensis* |
| White-breasted Kingfisher | *Halcyon smyrnensis* |
| Black-capped Kingfisher | *Halcyon pileata* |
| **Bee-eaters** | *Meropidae* |
| Blue-cheeked Bee-eater | *Merops superciliosus* |
| Blue-tailed Bee-eater | *Merops philippinus* |
| Green Bee-eater | *Merops orientalis* |
| **Rollers** | *Coraciidae* |
| Kashmir Roller | *Coracias garrulus* |
| Indian Roller | *Coracias benghalensis* |
| **Hoopoes** | *Upupidae* |
| Hoopoe | *Upupa epops* |
| **Hornbills** | *Bucerotidae* |
| Grey Hornbill | *Tockus birostris* |

# PICIFORMES

| **Barbets** | *Capitonidae* |
|---|---|
| Small Green Barbet | *Megalaima viridis* |
| Crimson-breasted Barbet or Coppersmith | *Megalaima haemacephala indica* |

| | |
|---|---|
| **Wrynecks, Woodpeckers** | *Picidae* |
| Wryneck | *Jynx torquilla* |
| Lesser Golden-backed Woodpecker | *Dinopium benghalense* |
| Yellow-fronted Pied Woodpecker | *Picoides mahrattensis* |
| Northern Pigmy Woodpecker | *Picoides nanus* |

## PASSERIFORMES

| | |
|---|---|
| **Pittas** | *Pittidae* |
| Indian Pitta | *Pitta brachyura* |
| **Larks** | *Alaudidae* |
| Red-winged Bush Lark | *Mirafra erythroptera* |
| Ashy-crowned Finch-Lark | *Eremopterix grisea* |
| Rufous-tailed Finch-Lark | *Ammomanes phoenicurus* |
| Short-toed Lark | *Calandrella cinerea* |
| Sand Lark | *Calandrella raytal* |
| Yarkand Crested Lark | *Galerida cristata magna* |
| Crested Lark | *Galerida cristata chendoola* |
| Sykes's Crested Lark | *Galerida deva* |
| Skylark | *Alauda arvensis* |
| Eastern Skylark | *Alauda gulgula* |
| **Martins, Swallows** | *Hirundinidae* |
| Indian Collared Sand Martin | *Riparia riparia* |
| Plain Sand Martin | *Riparia paludicola* |
| Dusky Crag Martin | *Hirundo concolor* |
| Western Swallow | *Hirundo rustica rustica* |
| Eastern Swallow | *Hirundo rustica gutturalis* |
| Wire-tailed Swallow | *Hirundo smithii* |
| Indian Cliff Swallow | *Hirundo fluvicola* |
| Striated Swallow | *Hirundo daurica* |
| **Pipits, Wagtails** | *Motacillidae* |
| Olive-backed Pipit | *Anthus hodgsoni* |
| Tree Pipit | *Anthus trivialis* |
| Richard's Pipit | *Anthus novaeseelandiae richardi* |
| Paddyfield Pipit | *Anthus novaeseelandiae waitei* |
| Tawny Pipit | *Anthus campestris* |
| Blyth's Pipit | *Anthus godlewskii* |
| Hodgson's Pipit | *Anthus roseatus* |
| Brown Rock Pipit | *Anthus similis* |
| Water Pipit | *Anthus spinoletta* |
| Forest Wagtail | *Motacilla indica* |
| Grey-headed Yellow Wagtail | *Motacilla flava thunbergi* |
| Blue-headed Yellow Wagtail | *Motacilla flava beema* |
| Black-headed Yellow Wagtail | *Motacilla flava melanogrisea* |
| Yellow-headed Wagtail | *Motacilla citreola citreola* |
| Black-backed Yellow-headed Wagtail | *Motacilla citreola calcarata* |
| Grey Wagtail | *Motacilla cinerea* |
| Pied or White Wagtail | *Motacilla alba* |
| Large Pied Wagtail | *Motacilla maderaspatensis* |
| **Cuckoo-Shrikes, Minivets** | *Campephagidae* |
| Common Wood Shrike | *Tephrodornis pondicerianus* |
| Black-headed Cuckoo-Shrike | *Coracina melanoptera* |

| | |
|---|---|
| Scarlet Minivet | *Pericrocotus flammeus* |
| Short-billed Minivet | *Pericrocotus brevirostris* |
| Small Minivet | *Pericrocotus cinnamomeus* |
| White-bellied Minivet | *Pericrocotus erythropygius* |
| **Bulbuls** | *Pycnonotidae* |
| Red-whiskered Bulbul | *Pycnonotus jocosus* |
| White-cheeked Bulbul | *Pycnonotus leucogenys* |
| Red-vented Bulbul | *Pycnonotus cafer* |
| White-browed Bulbul | *Pycnonotus luteolus* |
| **Ioras** | *Irenidae* |
| Common Iora | *Aegithina tiphia* |
| Marshall's Iora | *Aegithina nigrolutea* |
| **Shrikes** | *Laniidae* |
| Grey Shrike | *Lanius excubitor* |
| Bay-backed Shrike | *Lanius vittatus* |
| Pale Brown Shrike | *Lanius collurio* |
| Rufous-backed Shrike | *Lanius schach* |
| Brown Shrike | *Lanius cristatus* |
| **Robins, Chats, Thrushes** | *Turdidae* |
| Rubythroat | *Luscinia calliope* |
| Bluethroat | *Luscinia svecica* |
| Magpie-Robin | *Copsychus saularis* |
| Black Redstart | *Phoenicurus ochruros* |
| Brown Rock Chat | *Cercomela fusca* |
| Collared Bush Chat | *Saxicola torquata* |
| Pied Bush Chat | *Saxicola caprata* |
| Isabelline Wheatear | *Oenanthe isabellina* |
| Desert Wheatear | *Oenanthe deserti* |
| Black Wheatear | *Oenanthe leucura* |
| Indian Robin | *Saxicoloides fulicata* |
| Blue-headed Rock Thrush | *Monticola cinchlorhynchus* |
| Blue Rock Thrush | *Monticola solitarius* |
| Orange-headed Ground Thrush | *Zoothera citrina* |
| Tickell's Thrush | *Turdus unicolor* |
| Grey-winged Blackbird | *Turdus boulboul* |
| Black-throated Thrush | *Turdus ruficollis* |
| **Babblers** | *Timaliidae* |
| Yellow-eyed Babbler | *Chrysomma sinensis* |
| Common Babbler | *Turdoides caudatus* |
| Large Grey Babbler | *Turdoides malcolmi* |
| Jungle Babbler | *Turdoides striatus* |
| **Warblers** | *Silviidae* |
| Cetti's Warbler | *Cettia cetti* |
| Moustached Warbler | *Acrocephalus melanopogon* |
| Red-headed Fantail Warbler | *Cisticola exilis* |
| Streaked Fantail Warbler | *Cisticola juncidis* |
| Rufous-fronted Longtail Warbler | *Prinia buchanani* |
| Indian Wren Warbler | *Prinia subflava* |
| Ashy Longtail Warbler | *Prinia socialis* |
| Tailor Bird | *Orthotomus sutorius* |
| Temminck's Grasshopper Warbler | *Locustella lanceolata* |
| Thick-billed Warbler | *Acrocephalus aedon* |

| | |
|---|---|
| Indian Great Reed Warbler | *Acrocephalus stentoreus* |
| Blyth's Reed Warbler | *Acrocephalus dumentorum* |
| Blunt-winged Warbler | *Acrocephalus concinens* |
| Paddyfield Warbler | *Acrocephalus agricola* |
| Booted Warbler | *Hippolais caligata* |
| Orphean Warbler | *Sylvia hortensis* |
| Indian Whitethroat | *Sylvia communis* |
| Lesser Whitethroat | *Sylvia curruca blythi* |
| Hume's Lesser Whitethroat | *Sylvia curruca althaea* |
| Desert Warbler | *Sylvia nana* |
| Brown Leaf Warbler or Chiff-chaff | *Phylloscopus collybita* |
| Tytler's Leaf Warbler | *Phylloscopus tytleri* |
| Tickell's Leaf Warbler | *Phylloscopus affinus* |
| Grant's Leaf Warbler | *Phylloscopus subaffinus* |
| Radde's Leaf Warbler | *Phylloscopus schwarzi* |
| Olivaceous Leaf Warbler | *Phylloscopus griseolus* |
| Dusky Leaf Warbler | *Phylloscopus fuscatus* |
| Yellow-browed Leaf Warbler | *Phylloscopus inornatus* |
| Brooks's Leaf Warbler | *Phylloscopus subviridis* |
| Pallas's Leaf Warbler | *Phylloscopus proregulus* |
| Greenish Leaf Warbler | *Phylloscopus trochiloides* |
| Large Crowned Leaf Warbler | *Phylloscopus occipitalis* |
| **Flycatchers** | ***Muscicapidae*** |
| Red-breasted Flycatcher | *Ficedula parva* |
| White-browed Blue Flycatcher | *Ficedula superciliaris* |
| Blue-throated Flycatcher | *Cyornis rubicoloides* |
| Tickell's Blue Flycatcher | *Muscicapa tickelliae* |
| Verditer Flycatcher | *Muscicapa thalassina* |
| Grey-headed Flycatcher | *Culicicapa ceylonensis* |
| White-browed Fantail Flycatcher | *Rhipidura aureola* |
| Paradise Flycatcher | *Terpsiphone paradisi* |
| **Tits** | ***Paridae*** |
| Grey Tit | *Parus major* |
| **Nuthatches** | ***Sittidae*** |
| Chestnut-bellied Nuthatch | *Sitta castanea* |
| **Treecreepers** | ***Certhiidae*** |
| Spotted Grey Creeper | *Salpornis spilonotus* |
| **Flowerpeckers** | ***Dicaeidae*** |
| Thick-billed Flowerpecker | *Dicaeum agile* |
| Tickell's Flowerpecker | *Dicaeum erythrorhynchos* |
| **Sunbirds** | ***Nectariniidae*** |
| Purple Sunbird | *Nectarinia asiatica* |
| **White-eyes** | ***Zosteropidae*** |
| White-eye | *Zosterops palpebrosa* |
| **Buntings** | ***Emberizidae*** |
| Black-headed Bunting | *Emberiza melanocephala* |
| Red-headed Bunting | *Emberiza bruniceps* |
| White-capped Bunting | *Emberiza stewarti* |
| Reed Bunting | *Emberiza schoeniclus* |
| Crested Bunting | *Melophus lathami* |
| **Finches** | ***Fringillidae*** |
| Common Rosefinch | *Carpodacus erythrinus roseatus* |

| **Waxbills** | *Estrildidae* |
|---|---|
| Red Munia or Amadavat | *Estrilda amandava* |
| White-throated Munia | *Lonchura malabarica* |
| White-backed Munia | *Lonchura striata* |
| Spotted Munia | *Lonchura punctulata* |
| Black-headed Munia. | *Lonchura malacca* |
| **Sparrows, Weavers** | *Ploceidae* |
| Indian House Sparrow | *Passer domesticus indicus* |
| Kashmir House Sparrow | *Passer domesticus parkini* |
| Turkestan House Sparrow | *Passer domesticus bactrianus* |
| Spanish Sparrow | *Passer hispaniolensis* |
| Yellow-throated Sparrow | *Petronia xanthocollis* |
| Baya Weaver Bird | *Ploceus philippinus* |
| Black-throated Weaver Bird | *Ploceus benghalensis* |
| Streaked Weaver Bird | *Ploceus manyar* |
| **Mynas, Starlings** | *Sturnidae* |
| Black-headed or Brahminy Myna | *Sturnus pagodarum* |
| Rosy Pastor | *Sturnus roseus* |
| Starling | *Sturnus vulgaris* |
| Pied Myna | *Sturnus contra* |
| Common Myna | *Acridotheres tristis* |
| Bank Myna | *Acridotheres ginginianus* |
| **Orioles** | *Oriolidae* |
| Golden Oriole | *Oriolus oriolus* |
| Black-headed Oriole | *Oriolus xanthornus* |
| **Drongos** | *Dicruridae* |
| Black Drongo or King-Crow | *Dicrurus adsimilis* |
| White-bellied Drongo | *Dicrurus caerulescens* |
| **Tree Pies, Crows** | *Corvidae* |
| Tree Pie | *Dendrocitta vagabunda* |
| House Crow | *Corvus splendens* |
| Jungle Crow | *Corvus macrorhynchos* |

# Photocredits

**Thakur Dalip Singh**
ENDPAPERS, CONTENTS, PREFACE, Pgs. 12, 13 (top), 14, 15, 16, 49, 52, 53, 57, 60, 66, 70, 75, 78, 81 (top), 89, 92-93, 98, 99, 102, 103, 111, 118, 119, 122, 123 (bottom), 126-127
[COURTESY OF IMAGE VAULT]

**Rajpal Singh**
COVER, TITLE PAGE, Pgs. 13 (bottom), 18-19, 23 (bottom), 61, 64, 81 (bottom), 85, 96, 97, 110

**James Hancock**
Pgs. 22, 23 (top), 26, 27 (top), 35, 39 (bottom), 43, 56, 71, 74, 79

**M.Y. Ghorpade**
Pgs. 32, 36, 40, 68, 76, 86

**William S. Paton**
Pgs. 27 (bottom), 30-31, 84, 107, 114-115

**P. Evans**
Pgs. 34, 42, 46-47, 123 (top)

**P. Kapoor**
Pgs. 10-11

**Rupin Dang**
Pg. 106 (bottom)

**Mike Price**
Pg. 39 (top)

**M.M. Singh**
Pg. 67

**V.K. Sinha**
Pg. 87 [COURTESY OF IMAGE VAULT]

**Ashish Chandola**
Pg. 106 (top) [COURTESY OF R. FOTOMEDIA]

**Joanna Van Gruisen**
Pg. 88 [COURTESY OF R. FOTOMEDIA]